Window Boxes
and
Hanging Baskets

WINDOW BOXES
and
HANGING BASKETS

CLAIRE PHOENIX

PHOTOGRAPHS BY SPIKE POWELL AND GLYN BARNEY

CRESCENT BOOKS

New York • Avenel

For Em, Robert, Rupert and Holly

This 1996 edition is published by Crescent Books,
a division of Random House Value Publishing, Inc.,
40 Engelhard Avenue, Avenel, New Jersey 07001.

Crescent Books and colophon are trademarks of
Random House Value Publishing, Inc.

Random House
New York ● Toronto ● London ● Sydney ● Auckland

Printed and bound in Italy

A CIP catalog record for this book is available
from the Library of Congress.

ISBN 0-517-14304-6

8 7 6 5 4 3 2 1

CONTENTS

INTRODUCTION

The Smallest Garden

Creating your own hanging baskets and window boxes is the simplest way to try out all sorts of gardening – from alpines to strawberries, spring bulbs to tomatoes. With the minimum outlay you can achieve very satisfying results.

Whether you have gardened for years or have no garden at all, a hanging basket or window box is the ideal starting point. This book contains lots of ideas to show you just how different various combinations of classic plants can look – it's part of their beauty that they never have quite the same appearance twice. More importantly, I also hope to tempt you to try some more unusual combinations.

There are lots of gardening tips, plus clear, step-by-step photographs and key illustrations so that you will know exactly what to plant where.

There are sections on the vital elements of soil, watering and plant care. Ideas are given for more unusual containers, and for decorating containers with stenciling and liming.

Of course, you could limit your hanging

baskets and window boxes to a few warm summer months, and opt for the more obvious plants such as geraniums, impatiens and ivy, but there are many other lovely and easily grown plants to discover. Whether you have a difficult, shady spot to fill, or would like to try a more unusual wild flower window box, there are ideas here to tempt you.

There are also plans for the fall and winter, when, as gardens begin to die down, there is an even greater need for color in our lives. At this time, Christmas displays and wooden baskets can be used inside, or outside in a reasonably sheltered position.

This book caters to a wide range of gardening knowledge and experience, from ideas for children attempting their first baskets to stunning displays grown from seeds and cuttings. One section is devoted to single species baskets, which can be particularly effective, and another to foliage planting, which makes a refreshing contrast to brightly colored beds and borders.

Enjoy browsing through the various plans and do not be afraid of attempting something a little different – you are likely to be surprised and delighted with the results.

UNUSUAL WINDOW BOXES

From bicycle carriers to wooden baskets, watering cans to brightly colored plastic pots, there are more ways to arrange plants than in a traditional window box.

From pottery to plastic, stone to wrought iron, there are more types of window box than you can imagine. A stroll around a nearby garden center or along the streets of your hometown can give you ideas for the containers you would – or perhaps would not – like to use. You may come across a wonderful old lead window box or an excellent plastic reproduction. Each type of window box has its advantages and drawbacks. Stone is beautiful but extremely heavy, plastic is lightweight but not so attractive, and can age badly, cracking and yellowing. However, when planted, plastic can be indiscernible from, say, terracotta, and costs far less. Terracotta looks good, and, being heavier than plastic, is more stable. It is also porous, however, which means that the compost can dry out in hot weather, and it is not always frost-proof.

You may need to adjust your plans so that box and plants complement each other. There's no need always to opt for a ready-made box or basket. Be a little inventive, and perhaps use an old picnic basket to create an individual plant holder that will be greatly admired.

● Make the most of old galvanized watering cans by filling them with plants and arranging them along a sill. You will need to drill holes for drainage. Choose trailing plants such as these trailing petunia, "Surfinia," and verbena, although the taller clary sage stand up effectively.

● An old bicycle carrier makes a good window box, enhanced by the mass of geraniums. Line it with slit plastic, compost and slow-release fertilizer. Choose a sunny spot for geraniums, and water regularly in hot spells. Hang by the leather straps on screwed-in wire.

● A rustic log provides a harmonious container for year-round window box arrangements. Here, chrysanthemums, marguerites and the warm variegated foliage of a coleus provide late summer and early fall color.

● Fill an old wooden basket with a mass of soft color, and sit it on a sill, inside or out. Here fuchsias, impatiens (*Impatiens walleriana*), petunias and *Ageratum* mingle delicately with silver-leafed *Helichrysum petiolatum*.
Tip: Use plastic liner to keep the wood from rotting.

● A simple line-up of pots in nature's clashing colors provides a refreshing contrast to more organized arrangements. From left to right, heliotrope, rock rose, oxalis, impatiens, geraniums, marguerites, marigolds and plectranthus create a childlike array.

● Plant in an old beer crate by lining it first with slit plastic and then adding broken crockery and compost. This version had a slatted bottom but you may need to drill drainage holes. It is deep enough for a hydrangea, scabious, petunias and marigolds to bloom happily.

HANGING BASKETS WITH A DIFFERENCE

From old kettles to colanders, unusual baskets are tucked away in corners just waiting to be filled with flowers. Seek a change from the traditional wire basket.

The earliest type of hanging basket was made of simple wires strung together in a lattice pattern. Now there are a great many different types, from plastic bowls on chains, with a reservoir to aid watering, to ornate "bird cages" which make an attractive feature even when the basket is empty.

The most popular option is a plastic-coated wire basket which does not rust, unlike the earlier versions, and has plenty of spaces for planting from below. There are plastic versions of this type with vertical fins which make inserting plants even easier. There are also ready-made hanging balls which break in half and then clip together again, where, in the past, two standard baskets had to be wired together to form a sphere.

Wicker baskets can look extremely effective, but are best lined with plastic to prevent excessive leaching of water and compost. Unusual containers, such as colanders and kettles, make good hanging baskets, and are worth looking out for.

● Original cast-iron cauldrons, such as this, have been widely copied in lightweight plastic versions. If you are lucky enough to have an original, make sure your fasteners are secure as they are weighty. A blend of oxalis, geraniums, petunias and fuchsia creates a pleasing container.

● Make the most of an unusual basket – this one is made of green wire and bamboo – by planting harmonizing colors. The simple green and white theme of white *Dianthus* and variegated ivy is particularly striking, and does not detract from the container.

● Ready-made wall pots are available in glazed and unglazed pottery – they make good vacation souvenirs. This terracotta version has a design of grapes, and looks just right filled with oxalis, verbena and petunias.

● A three-tier, wire vegetable holder may be out of vogue in the kitchen, but makes an excellent hanging basket. Here three apricot portulaca, with their fat, waxy leaves, make an eyecatching trailing arrangement that thrives best in full sun. Using the same plant for each layer is effective.

● A metal colander makes a pretty and unusual hanging basket. With drainage holes ready made, you simply need to hang it, using strong wire or hook-on chains. Planted with trailing petunias and campanula to harmonize with the blue and white colander, it makes a picturesque corner.

● Hunt out an old kettle or oversize teapot for a more unusual hanging basket. Trailing plants such as creeping jenny, petunia and verbena combine with more upright marigolds and blue felicia for a colorful arrangement that makes passersby smile.

● Window boxes are cheerful on balconies where they please the small-scale gardener and passersby alike. Hanging baskets can look particularly attractive when color-balanced with boxes below. Here fuchsias, petunias, verbena and impatiens create a striking show.

● Dahlias at the doorstep, hanging balls of trailing geraniums (*P.* "Mini Cascade") and cascading fuchsias combine with myriad plants in the border to make this row of terraced cottages one of the prettiest exteriors seen – or rather hidden.

● A typical town house. Here gray brick and stonework have been lifted with bright window boxes of red geraniums (*P. hortorum* "Red Elite"). A basket of trailing begonias, fuchsias and geraniums links with a border of *Ageratum* and more geraniums.

● A simple, pale gray facade has been given a lift with a mass of trailing pink geraniums. To insure such a wonderful display, you need to begin early in the season, giving the plants a good start in a greenhouse if possible. A large, deep window box to retain moisture will also help.

CREATING AN IMPRESSION

Against any building backdrop, whether wood, brick, or stucco, window boxes and hanging baskets are a celebration of the season.

Wherever you live, a hanging basket or window box will make a lasting first impression on visitors.

This is your opportunity to create a welcoming windowbox or basket that says how much you care about your home. Decorating need not stop at immaculate paintwork – baskets and window boxes will soften the exterior of your home, and give it an inviting and perfectly finished appearance. A carefully tended window box or basket will bring pleasure to you and passersby for a whole season, and, with carefully chosen planting, can act as a link between your home and garden.

Before selecting any plants, consider the exterior of your home. Will your basket or window box be mounted against wood, brick, or stucco? Do you wish the colors of your plants to contrast or blend in? Could you plan a scheme to coordinate with the paintwork or other house features, or do you intend the plants to stand out in a bold display of color?

Take a look at your neighbors' gardens and houses. Do you wish to create a complete contrast, or do you wish to plant boxes and hanging baskets to blend in with the "look" of your street? Don't just think of the warm seasons. Lovely baskets and boxes can be planted for year-round enjoyment.

● In a riot of color, this one-storied house has been given a vibrant facelift with balls of impatiens and marigolds, baskets of geraniums and lobelia and a contrasting border of *Ageratum* and marigold that is vivid enough to stop you in your tracks.

● This unusual cast-iron window box of pink trailing geraniums would be appreciated from both inside and out. On each side of the garage entrance baskets containing four varieties of fuchsia, geraniums and lobelia brighten what could be an otherwise dull area.

● Two brimming baskets and a stunning bank of summer flowers lift these garages out of the ordinary. Petunias, pendulous fuchsias and marigolds subtly enhance the pink of the stucco walls, while softening the harder edges of the building.

● Strong pink trailing verbena and geraniums with stunning red impatiens and begonias are mixed with shades of lobelia (*Lobelia erinus* "Rosamund" and *L. e.* "Crystal Palace") to create a wonderful balance of color against this blue door.

● Glorious baskets of geraniums – both upright and trailing – petunias and lobelia. Prettily variegated Swedish ivy and the light foliage of helichrysum echo the pale green of the door. When hanging baskets by a door, be aware of the final "bulk" of the flowers in full bloom.

● A porch doorway is framed and softened with three baskets of geraniums, petunias, silvery helichrysum and lobelia. The color scheme is followed through at ground level with wooden tubs filled with flowers in colors that complement the bright shades of the baskets.

MAKING AN ENTRANCE

Create a welcoming first impression with brimming baskets hanging by your door.

If the windows are the eyes of your home, then your doorway is its mouth and voice. The secret of these planting schemes is that they have all been carefully chosen to flatter the doorway and its surroundings. From a double garage to an unused cellar, all doorways benefit from complementary color.

One of the joys of small-scale gardening is that, even when using similar plants, each basket and box is totally individual. The popular summer annuals – geraniums, petunias, fuchsias, impatiens and lobelia – are each time arranged in differing proportions, using different varieties. Employing blue-and-pink-toned plants to echo a door color makes an attractive arrangement that is easy on the eye.

Contrasting foliage plants add more interest, with the result that each basket is unique, and can be planned to reflect the character of your home. Obviously, it is important to think ahead a little before fastening hanging baskets by a doorway. A basket that has just been planted takes up no more room than its own diameter. When in full bloom, however, the total area it occupies is considerably more. For this reason, do not set the baskets too close to the doorway; otherwise the petals and foliage will be damaged by people brushing past.

● An unused doorway looks inviting with this collection of pots and a bright hanging basket of marigolds, brachycome, verbena, lobelia and *Bidens aurea* beneath the arch of a leafy wisteria. Make sure that you do not let foliage and plants obscure a background feature too much.

● A light-colored wooden door is given a fresh country feel when flanked by two colorful baskets. Lobelia, fuchsia, geraniums, and gold brachycome combine with the garden to create a welcoming entrance. Without the baskets, this doorway might look rather severe.

WINDOWS

Plant your window box to make the most of your window or to change its character completely.

Some windows will benefit more from hanging baskets and window boxes than others. If your house is close to the road, has little or no front garden and many passersby, a basket or window box can have a noticeable effect, and will be much admired.

Even if your window box is for your eyes alone, you will receive months of pleasure for relatively little outlay. It is worth planning the position of your hooks and boxes before you start. Take note of successful arrangements in your area, and you will discover which sizes and combinations work best. You may find that window boxes would work better above, rather than below, your window, provided they are easy to water.

One long window box is less likely to dry out than two smaller ones. You may wish to have a number of window boxes or baskets arranged vertically rather than horizontally. Symmetrical baskets often work well, although it is rare to see such symmetry in nature! A number of small hanging baskets will need a great deal of care because these tend to dry out quickly; fewer, larger baskets may be a better choice, and watering will prove less of a chore than with many small baskets.

Just as in art, everyone's taste in flowers differs. You may wish for single-color planting, mixed colors, or something completely different such as vegetables. Consider the next section, on season, size, soil and situation, before you make your final decision.

● Pretty baskets on each side of a traditional bow window differ in size and planting schemes. Nasturtiums and geraniums on the left link with petunias in the barrel below, and contrast with fuchsias, petunias, and trailing ivy in the opposite basket.

● Strongly shaped planting suits an individual window. The spiky cordyline has been surrounded with holly, cyclamen, gold-tinged euonymus, ivy and silvery *Senecio maritima*, all of which will survive the winter in a sheltered spot, and continue to provide interesting foliage.

● A classic bay window with deep sills has the advantage of three separate positions for window boxes. You could opt for a coordinated scheme, or, as here, aim for three completely different planting arrangements of ivy, red geraniums and marigolds with lobelia and helichrysum.

● Sometimes delicate planting schemes can be the most effective, especially when you have taken into consideration the background – in this case an old brick and half-timbered building. Here a mix of the palest pink impatiens and mauve and white lobelia works well.

● White stucco makes an excellent backdrop for a traditional mix of geraniums, begonia and lobelia. The unusually positioned boxes above the window link well with the ground-level planting and the pristine, newly painted white lattice above and below.

● A cascading window box links first-floor and basement windows. Three geraniums – a double bright red (*Pelargonium hortorum* "Gustave Emich"), a bicolored pink and a small white geranium – sit above purple verbena and deep pink "Surfinia" (trailing petunia).

THINGS TO THINK ABOUT

Before you rush out and buy a basket or box and some colorful plants to fill it, there are a few things worth remembering. They could be called the four S's – season, size, soil and site – all factors worth considering, whether you are planting your first basket or trying something completely new.

Season

It used to be assumed that hanging baskets and window boxes were just for the warm summer

● Be aware of the size of your house in proportion to the size of basket. Too small a basket, such as this one of pink and white diascia, looks lost, whereas a basket of the correct size and planting will enhance your home, and appear to be in balance.

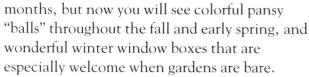

months, but now you will see colorful pansy "balls" throughout the fall and early spring, and wonderful winter window boxes that are especially welcome when gardens are bare.

Evergreen foliage can be attractive in itself – with golden tones and berried plants adding extra brilliance. Later in the year, some plants may be discarded, and flowering plants added.

Size

Do keep in mind the size of your window when buying or making a window box. Those that are too small can look rather drab and out of place. The larger and deeper your box, the easier it will be to maintain healthy plants. A larger box can hold more soil, and therefore retains more moisture when you water, thus avoiding one of the major problems, that of drying out.

Think about buying a basket a size larger than you had first planned – 12-inch baskets are really only suitable for very small arrangements, and will dry out very quickly indeed. A 14-inch basket is a good general standard, while a 16-inch basket will give you a full and professional-looking display. The larger baskets can be very heavy when the soil is wet, so make sure that your fasteners are strong and secure.

Soil

Some plants need a particular soil type to survive. Heathers, for example, like an acid soil, and will quickly die in soil that is full of lime. Most plants are quite happy in a multi-purpose potting compost, but it is worth checking, either with your garden center or in the plants section at the back of this book (see page 104).

Some plants, such as alpines, need a well-drained soil which can be achieved by mixing in horticultural gravel. If you are planting them in a

● A box of hot summer color that thrives in a sunny spot: marguerites, marigolds, petunias, helichrysum, lobelia, geraniums, flossflower and felicia all love the sun, whereas the fuchsias and impatiens would do equally well in semi-shade.

window box, place a layer of broken clay pots or pebbles over the holes in the bottom of the box to insure adequate drainage.

Most plants dislike sitting in water, and if you are worried about overwatering, it is worth layering charcoal in the bottom layer of soil to prevent mold and mildew. You will find further information about compost types on page 100.

Site

It is easy to assume that hanging baskets and window boxes are best situated in a sunny spot; however, many plants, such as impatiens, fuchsias and pansies, will flower happily in the shade, and numerous evergreens will give a verdant display in shady spots all year round.

Success often depends on the position of the basket or box. Check whether plants prefer a sunny, shady or semi-shady position (see page 104).

● These pink and white ornamental cabbages and heathers create a living collage for the winter months, but will not survive long without ericaceous (acidic) compost.

● Here the paler green of spotted laurel and the darker green of conifers form the basis of an attractive winter scheme – cyclamen will survive among the warmth of city buildings, and are offset by silver *Artemisia absinthium* and variegated ivy.

WHERE TO HANG A BASKET

The most obvious place for a basket is by a doorway – and with good reason. It can be seen whenever you enter the house, and will be enjoyed by neighbors and casual passersby.

However, there are many other areas that benefit greatly from a colorful display of baskets. Fences and walls, sheds and garages all become attractive features when festooned with flowers and foliage.

You can make your own holders for baskets – such as the post with brackets and the trellis shown here. Or simply use regular brackets well fixed into the wall.

Consider where your basket will be most appreciated. An herb basket by the back door will be in easy reach, and will bring the scent of aromatic herbs into your kitchen.

Try to plant according to the position of your basket. Choose sun-lovers for a sunny site, and plants tolerant of shade for cooler spots.

Wherever your basket is to be hung, check that it is not going to hit anyone on the head. Baskets can be extremely heavy when full and well watered.

Do insure that your basket is not going to be a nuisance to pedestrians – if it is going to hang over a sidewalk, set the brackets higher, and use a pulley system for watering.

● Two rows of baskets along a fence disguise what could be a boring area of the garden, and give it a totally different feel. *Lobelia erinus* in shades of purple, lilac, white and the less common, deep carmine "Rosamund" vie for space with marigolds, pansies, alyssum and white petunias.

● Create a striking basket of pastel color using one simple variety. Here impatiens (*Impatiens walleriana*) hung above a doorway combine tones of pink, white and lilac planted all around the basket to give a ball effect.

● Transform a dull brick wall with a trellis of hanging baskets. Here brilliant geraniums (*Pelargonium hortorum* "Paul Crampel" and "Queen of the Whites") are intermingled with petunias and marigolds, underslung with red and blue lobelia interspersed with variegated ivies.

● Fuchsias and impatiens would thrive in a shady spot – such as under this tree – but lobelia requires some sun, so the basket would need to be moved for some part of the day. Lilac, purple and masses of white lobelia combine to create a cool and delicate spherical basket.

● A fence post or ready-made bracket holder creates a stunning area of the garden when holding two brimming hanging baskets. Variegated petunias, white alyssum, geraniums, nasturtiums and marigolds make a show when mingled with mixed shades of lobelia.

● Make the entrance to your house welcoming with brimming baskets of color hung on each side of the door. Delicate pink shades of tobacco plant, lobelia and pale green helichrysum coordinate with the stronger pinks of "Surfinia," impatiens and fuchsia in the other basket.

21

● Symmetrical baskets of trailing ivy-leaf geraniums (*Pelargonium peltatum* "Galilee"). To create a spherical effect, two baskets have been planted separately and then wired together. This shows how baskets can contrast effectively with your wall color, rather than blending in.

● A striking purple and stained-glass door is set off to perfection with a hanging basket of petunias, geraniums and lobelia, with trailing ivy, in harmonious shades of pink, green and lilac, backed by rambling clematis bearing purple flowers that match the shade of the door.

● It's tempting to echo the colors of your garden in your window boxes, but here a cool planting scheme of green foliage would simply fade into obscurity. Instead, a bright arrangement of marigolds, impatiens and petunias provides a refreshing contrast.

● Five pots of vibrant zinnias have extra impact when used *en masse* between tomato-red window shutters. Do not be afraid to employ bold blocks of color. Try veering away from standard arrangements of pastel colors, and you are likely to be surprised and delighted with the results.

COLOR BALANCE

From coordination to creative contrast, the plants you use in your boxes and baskets should be chosen carefully. Plan them to link with your house or garden, and the result will be tastefully artistic.

The colors you choose for your planting schemes are your own personal area of design, even on such a small scale, so it is worth trying to imagine the effects you hope to achieve, rather than just picking up a random assortment of plants at your garden center, and hoping that they will all work together "somehow."

First, look at the exterior of your home. Are there colors you can pick up on, e.g., in the door or window frames? Are there plants in the bed below the window, which you would like to echo in your window box or hanging basket?

This is not to say that a mixed selection of plants cannot look particularly effective. Indeed, most baskets that you will see contain a mixture of colors. By studying other baskets, you will see that some of the most effective are those that have been planned to coordinate with, or make a contrast to, the house, another window box or each other.

Plan ahead. If your paintwork or masonry needs freshening up, do it *before* you hang baskets or attach boxes. Of course, if you are thinking of repainting, you can always make your new paintwork match your boxes and baskets.

● A cascading basket of pendulous fuchsias and Swedish ivy echoes and emphasizes the pink wall. Here hybrid petunias, geraniums and variegated pinks on the windowsills link with the healthy hydrangea and miniature roses below to stunning effect.

● Numerous shades of yellow and orange plants work well together, and contrast attractively here with the green foliage and paintwork. Dahlias, marigolds, pansies and celosia coordinate beautifully with variegated ivies, helichrysum and the rudbeckia and sunflowers below.

23

● An array of these feather duster plants would brighten up any corner. Commonly known as cockscombs (*Celosia amaranthaceae*), they come in red, pink, yellow and salmon, and look amusingly pert with their crested blooms. They do not grow very tall, so are ideal for window boxes.

● A striking combination of marigolds, monkey flower, chrysanthemums, geraniums and petunias. Take a closer look to spot the blues of felicia and campanula, the white marguerites and deep red lobelia – the details which give the arrangement depth.

HOT COLORS – BRIGHT IDEAS

Make the most of nature's brilliance with a basket or window box in vibrant colors that cheer and inspire. Choose from a profusion of begonias to a cascade of mixed summer color.

Many of the plants that enjoy the heat of summer come in a range of hot and sultry colors. From begonias and the fiery feather dusters of cockscombs, to luminous marigolds and bright geraniums, their brilliance proclaims that summer has arrived at last.

Many daisy-like plants, including Cape marigold (*Dimorphotheca*), gazanias, zinnias and helichrysum, open up in brilliant sunshine. Others that particularly enjoy direct light and warmth are petunias, pinks, miniature roses and verbena. Direct sunlight can, of course, be terribly fierce and drying. Some plants will need watering more than once a day, and perhaps moving to a shady spot for a few hours to avoid the worst of the sun's rays.

Succulent plants, such as portulaca and flowering cacti, are designed to survive well in hot conditions, storing water in their fleshy leaves.

Plants sited in very hot places will need plenty of water. Avoid getting water on leaves or petals as the tiny drops of water act like magnifying glasses in strong sunlight, and will cause the leaves or petals to burn.

● For the first bright, heartwarming colors of the year, you can't fail to please with ranunculus – wonderful peony-like plants from the buttercup family. These are available from early spring in rich single colors and more delicate whites with pink edging, and will flower until late summer.

● In return for rich, moist potting compost, begonias will reward you with vibrant color. Choose the smaller blooms of the low-growing varieties, such as *Begonia multiflora*, for window boxes, and do not plant outside until the frosts are over. Here, a terracotta pot adds to the warm effect.

● The apricot yellow of a pendulous begonia is given extra warmth by the proximity of a double pink impatiens. Purple brachycome and pale pink lobelia combine with a deep red, clustered fuchsia (*F.* "Thalia") to make this a harmoniously colorful basket.

● Luminous trailing begonias (*Begonia semperflorens*), French marigolds (*Tagetes patula* "Goldfinch") and large clusters of purple lobelia (*Lobelia erinus* "Crystal Palace") combine to provide an eye-catching window box that will remain a profusion of color throughout the summer.

25

● Create a miniature garden of soft colors in a window box. A tiny privet (*Ligustrum*) sits beside a trellis "fence." Miniature roses grow among geraniums and parsley. Trailing bugle (*Ajuga*) and euonymus soften the line of the box.

● Delicate shades of an unusual woolly lavender (*Lavandula lanata*) combine with the cool greens and creams of variegated sage, ivy and a small-leafed helichrysum (*H.* "Roundabout") to create a window box that would give off a delicious scent when brushed past.

COOL CREATIONS

Aim for subtle, calming colors – greens, yellows, pinks and whites – for baskets and window boxes that suggest peace and tranquillity. Blend them together for a harmonious display, choosing a range of delicate shades from the same color palette.

In contrast to many of the fiery displays of high summer, it can be particularly refreshing to cast your eye over something a little more subtle. There are many wonderful foliage plants which tend to be ignored, or used solely as a backdrop. However, when used together, these can look sophisticated and quite different in a cool, quiet way.

Many herbs have an interesting leaf shape which makes them useful both artistically and for culinary purposes. Flowering thyme, the soft "rabbit ears" of sage, lavenders, and the feathery foliage of fennel give textured appeal as well as the added bonus of a Mediterranean fragrance wafting through the air.

Most of the silver-leafed plants, including cineraria or dusty miller (*Senecio*), need more sun to keep their color than might be imagined, but are particularly rewarding.

Some miniature roses can be obtained in very sweet, soft colors, as can a whole range of wild flowers.

• The arching stems of this attractive silver-leafed chamomile (*Anthemis punctata*) reach skyward, and create an attractively feathered hanging basket. An upright fuchsia (*F.* "Sunray") and dusty miller (*Senecio maritima cirrhus*) keep the scheme within similar cool tones.

• In contrast to many brightly colored window boxes, the soft yellows and whites of pansies, marguerites and impatiens, and the subtle blues of felicia and spurred *Diascia cordata* offer a refreshingly natural look. These plants would enjoy a position in semi-shade.

• For a simple but effective winter window box, purple cineraria (*Senecio hybridus*) surrounded by evergreen foliage – laurel, spotted laurel and a star-shaped ivy (*Hedera helix* "Pittsburgh") – makes a striking combination. The bold cineraria flowers for many winter months.

• For an interesting foliage basket that also produces pale blue flowers from mid-spring to early summer, bugle (*Ajuga reptans* "Burgundy Glow") is a good choice. The leaves are wine red with white and pink shading, and this evergreen alpine will grow happily in sun or deep shade.

27

● Many plants that may seem too tall for window boxes also come in dwarf varieties. These blue dwarf delphiniums look particularly attractive against a lemon-washed wall with the green of the foliage echoed in the window box. They flower from late spring to early summer.

● Miniature tête à tête narcissi herald the arrival of spring, their strong, fresh, yellow heads nodding in the breeze against verdant standard and attractively variegated ivies. Plant the ivies in the fall with daffodil bulbs below and winter pansies above.

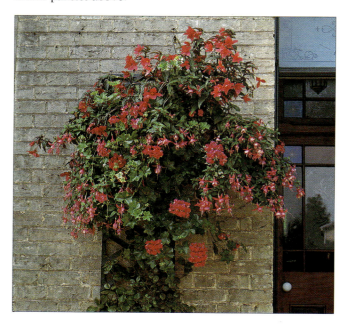

● A mass of trailing pink geraniums (*Pelargonium* "Mini Cascade") provides welcome color on a smart city street. The black of the door and shutters contrasts sharply with the soft pinks of the hanging basket. Geraniums are ideal for hanging baskets as they survive with little water.

● An ever-popular mix of pendulous fuchsia, begonia and trailing geraniums will win favor through being prolific and striking, although not without some effort. Fuchsias are particularly demanding of water. This basket is suitable for a semi-shady position.

SINGLE-COLOR PLANTING

For baskets and window boxes with the greatest impact, it is hard to top the effect of single-color planting. Hanging "balls" or overflowing window boxes of one flower or color type never fail to catch the eye.

It is extremely easy to push a cart around a nursery or garden center, picking up trays of plants that catch your eye, perhaps even buying two or three new varieties if you are feeling adventurous. The results, however, may not always be as impressive as you might hope. Take a look in other carts, and you will see that some people are planning an all-blue scheme, or one of white and green only. Even before planting, you can see how well colors of a similar hue work together, while a mixture can look garish and jumbled.

Take a tip from the experts, and plan your color scheme before you venture out. Make notes from year to year of successful and rewarding schemes, and keep the plant tags to remind you. From sunny yellow daffodils with simple green foliage to an all-white daisy, or all-blue lobelia, ball, there are myriad ways to use a group of plants within one area of the color palette. The results can be most effective.

● For a strikingly pretty ball of daisies, follow the planting instructions for the pansy ball on page 78. If bedding plants are not available, simply make larger holes for more mature plants. The marguerites will fill out, and, with regular deadheading, will bloom all summer long.

● A wicker hamper makes an attractive window box when lined with slit plastic to prevent compost from leaking out. Here a mass of orange chrysanthemums provides a block of warm color that will flower from late summer to early fall in a sunny spot.

● Green and white schemes look effective – clean and modern, romantically soft and pretty – especially when many plants are used. Here hybrid impatiens, pinks (*Dianthus* "Snowflake"), forget-me-not (*Myosotis* "White Ball"), ivy and plectranthus are artistically combined.

● You can grow herbs on a sunny windowsill, but this basket would need to spend some time outside too. Fennel, sorrel, parsley, mint, chives and thyme would provide for many of your cooking requirements, and the mingled trailing foliage looks particularly attractive.

● This relatively new fuchsia variety, *Fuchsia* "Autumnale," has wonderful leaf coloring, and creates enough foliage interest to make a striking hanging basket on its own. However, it also produces bright pink flowers in summer and fall, and enjoys a shady position.

● As an alternative to ivy, plectranthus is rapidly gaining in popularity for both hanging baskets and window boxes. Its attractive variegated leaf and natural trailing habit make it an ideal backdrop to many planting schemes. Plectranthus also looks quite dramatic when used alone.

SHADES OF GREEN

Rethink your attitude towards foliage schemes – the subtleties of leaf structure can be more fascinating than the most colorful planting arrangement.

When planning a hanging basket or window box, many of us instinctively opt for the latest trend in colors – recently blue, pink and purple have had a revival, whereas ten years ago it was orange and yellow. Looking, however, at some of the window boxes used by commercial properties, such as hotels, stores and offices, proves that there are valuable lessons to be learned. Here a backdrop of evergreens, such as conifers and ivies, is used all year round, interplanted with primroses and pansies in spring, geraniums and begonias in summer, chrysanthemums in the fall and cineraria in winter, all prolific-flowering plants of their season, which look good against a green backdrop.

It is unfair to place foliage plants in the sole role of backdrop to flowering planting schemes, however, as many non-flowering plants are very rewarding in their own right.

From the luxuriant colors of coleus to the deep burgundy brown of Japanese maple (*Acer palmatum*), there are innumerable foliage plants which go extremely well together, or will create an unusual hanging basket when used entirely alone.

● A multitude of plants have been chosen here, particularly for their unusual foliage. From beets to nasturtiums, zonal geraniums to spurge, pick-a-back plant (*Tolmiea*) to periwinkle, the different leaf structures look wonderful when grouped in a window box.

● For an attractive set of green foliage plants that is also useful, try keeping herbs on a windowsill near the kitchen door. Flowering thyme, variegated sage, curled parsley and tarragon jostle happily for space, and will give an aromatic bonus too when carried on the warm summer air.

SINGLE PLANT TYPES OR SPECIES

Simplify your ideas and you will be surprised by the results. Individual plant schemes have a great deal of poise and horticultural panache.

While you can achieve a planting scheme of great impact by using a number of different plants within one range of color, the most striking baskets and window boxes, especially from a distance, are those containing a single species, variety or plant type.

Whether you choose a window box of begonias or a basket of impatiens, the results are likely to be impressive. Check pages 18 and 19 to insure that you have taken into account the four S's – site, season, soil and situation. Impatiens will thrive in a shady spot, but some plants need more careful siting. Different varieties of pansies bloom happily throughout the seasons, but not all plants are so happy all year round. Some plants, such as the hydrangeas shown here, are rarely seen in baskets, perhaps because they require ericaceous (lime-free) compost or large amounts of water, and possibly because they can grow fairly large, so that most people think of them as a garden shrub.

The easiest single plant types to grow must be geraniums, more varieties of which are being bred all the time. As single planting schemes, they are hard to better.

● Pansy balls make rewarding hanging baskets, bringing bright color to cheer the winter months, and then again through spring and summer. There are numerous varieties available including this cheerful mixture (*Viola* "Universal" mixed). (See the instructions on page 78.)

● Bold geraniums (*Pelargonium hortorum* "Red Elite") brighten the gray brick of a typical townhouse. Geraniums flower best in a sunny spot, and are easy to grow as they can survive with less water than many plants, although occasional feeding will boost the display.

● Linking two baskets, one hanging, one used on a windowsill, with a similar color scheme, looks effective without being ostentatious. The ball of pink tradescantia – a recently developed plant – harmonizes well with the chrysanthemums – yet both have individual character.

● Create a stunning spherical basket using the color spectrum of one single species. Here impatiens (*Impatiens walleriana*) have been used to great effect by combining subtle tones of pink, white and lilac planted through the basket to give all-round growth.

● Enjoy a blue mophead hydrangea at close quarters by siting it in a window box with variegated ivies. You can buy the ericaceous compost which it needs to keep its color, or convert multi-purpose compost by adding a liquid solution, using powders available from garden centers.

● The palette of pink, white and purple shades found in these heathers (*Erica cineraria* "Moonstone White," *E. vagans* "Mrs D.F. Maxwell" and *Calluna vulgaris* "Silver Knight") combines well in a windowsill display. Heathers require ericaceous compost and moist conditions.

PLANTING AND PLANTING DESIGNS

Gardening on the small scale presented by window boxes and hanging baskets is the perfect opportunity to try out all sorts of planting ideas that you might not otherwise attempt.

From herb gardens to scented baskets, this is your chance to try out new arrangements with a specific theme in mind. Alpines, for instance, can soon be lost in a larger bed, but are easy to appreciate at eye level. Also, the free-draining environment that they most appreciate can readily be created.

You may have thought it would be fun to make a pansy ball, but were not quite sure how to go about it. The clear, step-by-step instructions given on page 78 will make the whole process less daunting.

Rather than producing just a simple basket of mixed flowers in summer, it is worth considering year-round planting schemes. Winter evergreens can be underplanted with spring bulbs, and then added to for colorful summer arrangements.

Edible plants in baskets and window boxes, such as strawberries and tomatoes, are ideal for those of us with little space. Their early flowers make them an attractive feature even before the fruits appear.

Whatever your interest, there are planting displays on the following pages to inspire you – if you have always yearned for a wild flower garden, or simply need to fill a shady corner, browse through these pages, and you will find schemes for all sites and seasons.

MAKING A WINDOW BOX

Begin by measuring and marking the position of the angle brackets, as shown. With the bradawl make holes, where marked, for each set of four screws. Insert the screws – an electric screwdriver makes the job much quicker. Insure that the last piece you add is a long side, and screw the brackets to this before attaching it to the box, because it can be difficult screwing both angles of the last brackets directly into the box.

Lime is dangerous to work with as it can cause caustic burns unless you wear thick gloves. If you do choose to use powdered lime, you will need to add water until you have a runny liquid. A similar effect can be achieved using white emulsion.

You may need to water the paint down until it is the consistency of light cream. Apply to all areas of the box, except the bottom. When dry, use a wire brush to remove paint until you are happy with the result. A certain amount of woodgrain should show through.

YOU WILL NEED
─────

3 × 2-inch stainless steel
angle brackets
3 pieces lumber 6 × 30 inches
2 pieces lumber 6 × 6 inches
32 ½-inch flathead wood screws
tape measure · pencil
screwdriver · bradawl

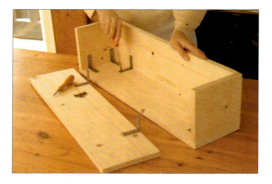

1 Follow the instructions in the main text for assembling the window box. Remember to drill holes in the bottom for drainage. Three holes at regular intervals should be sufficient for this size box. Increase the number if you are making a larger box.

2 If you are staining the box, rub in woodstain using a soft cloth. We chose a soft yellow to enhance our bronze stars and silver moon stencils, but almost any shade of brown or green would be certain to complement your floral arrangement.

3 Old, roughened wood is often best for showing off a limed effect. You will probably still need to rough up the grain with a wire brush, deepening the grooves along the straight of the grain. Some woodgrain should show through.

4 You can then stencil the limed trough using your chosen design, or plant it in its natural state without any further ornamentation. A coat of clear matte varnish will insure that your limed effect and stencil does not wash off in the rain.

Hand-painted window boxes and pots with limed and stenciled finishes.

Stenciling

Plastic stencils are widely available in craft stores, or you can make your own using an X-acto knife and stencil card. Quick-drying stencil paints are available, but regular emulsions can work just as well on wooden window boxes as long as a final coat of clear matte varnish is put on to seal in your design. If you use exterior paints, this will not be necessary.

You may have leftover household paints which you can use, or you might be able to obtain small sample pots that fit your intended scheme. Enamel paints in primary colors, and metallics intended for toy painting, are also suitable.

Many gardeners have artistic leanings, and you may be inspired to paint your own container, such as the watering can shown here. First paint your container in a base color, and let it dry completely. Then, after sketching your idea on paper, transfer it to the metal medium using suitable paints. For beginners, an abstract leaf shape would be easier than the scene shown here of swans on a lake. If this is the first time you have painted pots and containers, do not be too ambitious with your first attempts.

1 Using either plastic or terracotta pots, attach your stencil with masking tape, and apply the paint using a stencil brush. If stenciling a wooden window box, paint it in your base color, and let it dry thoroughly overnight.

2 If the paint tends to seep beneath the stencil on a plastic pot, it may be easier to outline the design using a wax pencil; then remove the stencil, and fill in with enamel paints using the smaller paintbrush.

3 You may wish to use just part of a larger stencil to create a coordinating theme. Bold blocks of primary colors work well, giving the effect of barge painting. Fine detail will only be seen close up so decide ahead where to put the pot.

YOU WILL NEED

1 quart base color exterior paint
– matte, silk or gloss (for box)
a stencil · masking tape · wax pencil · enamel or gloss paints stencil or thick-headed brushes fine brush for detailed work

QUICK TIPS

● Choose stencils that give bright blocks of color. These will look very effective from a distance.

● If paint runs beneath stencils on a plastic pot, outline the design in wax pencil, and then paint this.

● Do not be too ambitious with your first attempts unless you are sure of your artistic skills.

● If painting a window box, apply a painted base coat of one color, and let this dry overnight. Otherwise the stencil may smudge.

Springtime primroses in an ethnic, stenciled window box with hand-painted bargeware pots and a watering can.

PLANTING

Step by Step to Planting a Window Box

Just like hanging baskets, window boxes have a tendency to dry out, so some of these steps are specifically intended to counteract this problem.

The planting scheme itself can be varied to suit almost any colors you have in mind – there are plenty of ideas throughout the book – but we thought these bright oranges and blues made a refreshing change from more traditional colors. Hydrangeas make particularly good container plants provided the soil is ericaceous (acidic not alkaline) and they are kept well watered.

Tip: Charcoal scattered in the bottom will prevent container plants from becoming mildewed through overwatering.

YOU WILL NEED

a window box, e.g., wood, stone, plastic, terracotta
about 20 pounds ericaceous compost
broken clay pots or pebbles for base
plastic for lining
water-retaining granules
fertilizer granules
8 French marigolds · 6 African marigolds · 10 petunias
1 scabious · 1 hydrangea
a hand-operated or electric drill

1 Provide drainage holes in the bottom of the box – one every 6 inches. Cover the bottom inside with pottery or pebbles to prevent soil from leaching out. A plastic lining will prevent a wooden box from bowing through dampness.

2 Fill to one-third with compost (for most plants a multi-purpose variety is adequate, but the hydrangea will need ericaceous compost), adding a few handfuls of water-retaining granules. Sprinkle in the fertilizer.

3 Test run the position of the plants while still in their pots, then insert the hydrangea. Place the medium-sized scabious on the left. Add the African and French marigolds, and fill in with petunias. Fill with compost and water thoroughly.

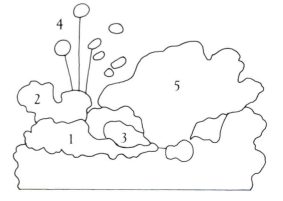

1 French marigolds
2 African marigolds
3 petunias
4 scabious
5 hydrangea

Plant a basic window box with a vibrant purple and orange theme using marigolds and a hydrangea.

Planting a Basic Hanging Basket

Here we aim to give you a "recipe" so that you can recreate the colorful summer basket opposite. Clear step-by-step photographs and instructions are provided, although they do not need to be followed to the letter. These plants are all popular for container gardening. However, should a particular plant be unavailable, your garden center will advise you of a suitable substitute.

We have used quite a large basket as the 10- and 12-inch versions hold too little compost, and tend to dry out quickly. Lack of water is the most common reason for unsuccessful hanging baskets. A liner made of plastic, fibrous matting or foam will help to retain water. "Self-watering" baskets are available, with a reservoir of water in the base, but these are generally made of plastic so plants cannot be pushed through the sides.

YOU WILL NEED

a plastic-coated wire basket
14 inches in diameter
5-pound bag of moss
10 pounds potting compost
fibrous/foam liner (optional) or
plastic cut to fit
1 trailing begonia
1 geranium · 1 pot verbena
1 pink impatiens
3 purple petunias
1 pot *Bidens aurea*
1 rock rose (*heliantheum*)
lobelia or pansies
watering can · trowel

1 First assemble your "ingredients." You may find it easier to put your basket on a bucket. Then plan the arrangement, with the tallest plants to the rear and the smallest, trailing plants around the edges, or inserted from below.

2 Line the basket with the moss, arranging it to cover the entire surface. Add the fibrous paper or foam liner, cutting holes for lower planting if the liner allows. Half-fill with compost. Remove plants from pots with care to avoid root damage.

3 Plant the begonia and geranium in the center. Thread lobelia and *Bidens aurea* roots into the bottom from the outside. Add the other plants, then fill up with potting compost right to the brim. Firm the plants, and water well.

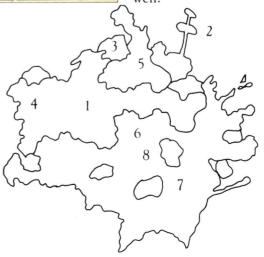

1 begonia
2 pelargonium
3 verbena
4 patience-plant
5 petunia
6 Bidens area
7 lobelia
8 rock rose

A basket of mixed summer flowers – begonia, petunia, verbena, impatiens, geranium and *Bidens aurea*.

Planting a Wall-Mounted Half-Basket

Wall-mounted baskets give a plain wall life and color. They take up less space than hanging baskets, and generally hold fewer plants. Because less compost is needed, they are, however, more prone to drying out, and need careful attention and regular watering.

Take into consideration the aspect of your wall when choosing plants. If it is a shady spot, you will find that geraniums will flower very little – opt for impatiens or fuchsias instead. A hot spot could make an ideal site for nasturtiums or other sun-loving plants.

Wall fastenings must be strong and secure. A full half-basket can be very heavy, and plants will be damaged should it fall.

It is worth lining the whole basket with polyethylene, especially the back, to prevent marks on your wall if you remove the basket during the winter.

YOU WILL NEED

a cast-iron or plastic-coated wire half-basket 14 inches in diameter
black plastic
10 pounds potting compost
5-pound bag of moss
2 geraniums – one trailing, one upright · Swedish ivy (*Nepeta*) · 6 lobelia
6 impatiens
1 creeping jenny (*Lysimachia nummularia*) · 1 red mimulus · 1 purple brachycome

1 Line the basket with black plastic, insuring the back wall is well protected. Fill with moss in front of the plastic, with the greenest part outermost, right up and over the top edge. Fill one-third with potting compost.

2 Sprinkle in granular fertilizer, and add another third of compost. Starting at one side, make cuts through the plastic liner with scissors, and insert the impatiens and lobelia, alternately, halfway down the basket to cover the sides.

3 Test your plan by placing the plants in the basket still in their pots. Place the upright geranium in the center and the trailing plants to the sides, with the Swedish ivy at the center front. Plant the basket, and firm the plants in.

1 *Swedish ivy*
2 *lobelia*
3 *impatiens*
4 *creeping jenny*
5 *mimulus*
6 *brachycome*
7 *geranium*

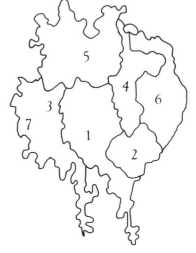

A colorful mix of geraniums, monkey flower and purple brachycome, with trailing lobelia and Swedish ivy.

SPRING FLOWERS
Easter Window Box

The best known spring-flowering bulbs – daffodils, tulips, grape hyacinths, iris and crocus – have earned their popularity by being hardy enough to withstand the cold winds and rain of early spring, and looking bright and colorful at a time of year when our gardens are only just coming into bud. However, many lesser-known bulbs are also worth trying, from the bell-like blue scillas to anemones.

As many spring bulbs, including crocus, daffodils and tulips, flower a few weeks after each other, many gardeners suggest surface planting with pansies or primroses in spring to give a constant display through which the bulbs can grow.

Our colorful window box is quite simple to plant, using trailing ivies, box and rosemary as a foliage base, with blue grape hyacinths underplanted in the fall, and primroses and polyanthus in yellow, pink and purple added later.

1 Arrange broken crockery to cover the drainage holes in the bottom of your window box. Fill the box to just below the rim with potting compost, and plant the grape hyacinth bulbs in clumps 1 inch below the surface in mid- to-late fall.

2 Plant with the foliage to the rear and the ivies trailing over the front and sides. Fill in with polyanthus and primroses as soon as you can find them, leaving space for the grape hyacinths to push through. Water the compost until it is damp but not waterlogged.

QUICK TIPS
• Drill holes in plastic troughs for drainage if none exist. Cover with crockery or pebbles, and fill to just below the brim with compost.
• Plant bulbs in rows or clusters, with the largest bulbs lowest. Cover with potting compost, water, and leave in a shady spot until late winter, keeping the soil moist. Then move to a sunny spot to encourage flowering.
• Add charcoal to prevent bulbs rotting.

YOU WILL NEED

1 window box about 30 inches long and 6 inches deep
broken clay pots or pebbles
multi-purpose potting compost
2 trailing ivies (*Hedera*)
2 pieces of green foliage
(e.g., rosemary, box)
3 primroses · 2 purple polyanthus · 25–30 grape hyacinth bulbs (*Muscari*)

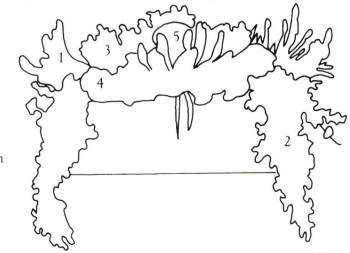

1 *grape hyacinth*
2 *ivy*
3 *green foliage*
4 *primrose*
5 *polyanthus*

Celebrate the coming of spring with blue grape hyacinths, fresh green rosemary and bright primroses.

Planting a Spring Hanging Basket

After the dull dark days of winter, it is cheering to see bulbs bursting into life, especially if you can position them in a basket near your front door.

If you intend using bulbs, you need to start planning in early fall and planting in mid-fall. Choose dwarf varieties for window boxes where possible, or you may find that the stems grow too long and the plants droop, or become too lanky and make the basket look uneven.

Alternatively, a visit to your local garden center in early to mid-spring can supply you with a colorful display of ready-grown bulbs that are hardy enough to withstand frosts and strong winds.

We chose a fairly traditional yellow mixture of tête à tête narcissi, dwarf tulips, a cowslip and a large primrose, and added color with pink and red daisies (*Bellis*) and clumps of grape hyacinth and scilla with its delicate, blue, star-shaped flowers.

YOU WILL NEED

a basket approximately
20 inches in diameter
thick plastic for liner
multi-purpose potting
compost · moss
1 cowslip (*Primula veris*)
tête à tête narcissi · 2 dwarf
tulips · 2 daisies (*Bellis*)
1 grape hyacinth (*Muscari*)
1 *Scilla sibirica* · 2 primroses
(*Primula*)
1 spurge (*euphorbia*)

1 Choose a basket with an interesting shape. Remember that it must be deep enough to hold the compost, and must have a very strong handle as it will be heavy when filled with fully grown plants and wet compost.

2 Line the basket with moss, then cut the plastic to shape for the liner. (Part of a compost bag will do.) Make slits to insure adequate drainage, and fill to two-thirds with potting compost. Decide which is to be the front of your basket.

3 Place the taller plants at the back. The cowslip, grape hyacinth and scilla will add a central splash of color and fragrance. Fill in with the primrose and daisies. Add extra compost where required.

1 cowslip
2 tête à tête narcissi
3 tulip
4 daisy
5 grape hyacinth
6 scilla
7 primrose
8 spurge

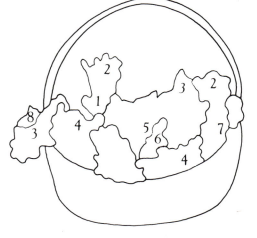

Create a pink, white and yellow theme with *Bellis* daisies, tête à tête narcissi and dwarf tulips.

HERBS

While a traditional herb garden can take up a great deal of space in a valuable sunny area of the garden, a window box or hanging basket takes up very little room, and can be positioned right outside the kitchen door.

The sometimes pungent scent given off by herbs can remind one of the Mediterranean, where many culinary herbs originate. Perhaps because of their origins, most herbs prefer a sunny spot and gritty, free-draining soil.

Few of us appreciate how pretty the foliage of a selection of herbs can be until we plant them together.

An Herb Window Box

For a small and stylish window box that you can keep close at hand on a kitchen windowsill, a simple metal container such as this is ideal. Most herbs need a sunny situation to do well, and this box will do equally well outside your kitchen door if conditions are right. We have used five of the most popular herbs.

1 Before you begin to plant them, try out the position of the plants first, keeping them in their pots, to judge where you wish them to trail, and how the leaf colors work best together. Place crockery in the bottom, and fill with gritted compost.

2 Plant the herbs, teasing the roots out gently to help them to acclimatize quickly. Train them to trail over the sides of the container if you wish. Water, taking care not to overwater. Cut herbs often to promote bushy growth.

QUICK TIPS
● Try to choose a spot that will make it easy for you to snip the herbs when preparing a meal.
● If you are using the window box inside, you will not need drainage holes but you will have to be careful when watering to insure that the soil does not become waterlogged.
● Remove flowerheads from chives, etc., to promote leaf growth.

YOU WILL NEED

a container, 12–20 inches long in metal, plastic or terracotta
1 chive (*Allium schoenoprasum*)
1 parsley (*Petroselinum*)
1 thyme (*Thymus*)
1 lemon balm (*Melissa officinalis*)
1 mint (*Mentha*)
crockery · medium potting mixture – half-gravel half-potting compost

1 *chives*
2 *parsley*
3 *thyme*
4 *lemon balm*
5 *mint*

Keep basic herbs, such as parsley, chives, thyme and mint, close at hand on your kitchen windowsill.

An Herb Cooking Guide

Chives: best used at the end of cooking. Snip over soups and sauces, mix with cream cheese over baked potatoes.

Fennel: the leaves taste of aniseed, and are good in tomato and fish sauces.

Mint: mostly used for mint sauce for lamb and with new potatoes. Also in tea.

Parsley: useful as an edible garnish, in stocks, and to freshen breath. Useful in sauces for fish, ham and egg. Freezes well.

Sorrel: a few handfuls of the leaves (about 1 cup) are enough for a delicious soup. Tastes like spinach.

Tarragon: a few sprigs for Béarnaise sauce or in wine vinegar for salad dressings.

Thyme: chopped in salad dressings – one teaspoonful. Or little sprigs in stocks and casseroles – especially beef. Dries well.

An Herb Basket

1 A plastic-lined wicker basket is ideal for an arrangement of herbs provided you make a few slits in the plastic before filling to provide drainage. A ratio of about half gravel and half compost gives the sort of free-draining environment herbs prefer.

2 Start by planting the taller sorrel and fennel in the center to the rear, then adding the chives, mint, tarragon and parsley around the edges. Keep the compost moist but not soggy – the gravel should insure that the compost is well drained.

QUICK TIPS

● Always used a free-draining compost – mix half gravel and half potting compost.
● Herbs enjoy a hot and sunny spot.
● Feed weekly during the summer months.
● Most plants will die off, and need replacing next spring.
● You could keep your herb basket hanging in the kitchen when it is well established. Herbs enjoy sunshine though, so hang it outside occasionally in a sunny spot.
● Do not worry if the herbs dry out a little; they will revive if trimmed and watered.
● Fennel grows to about 2 feet tall, so only plant it if you have enough room.

1 *fennel*
2 *sorrel*
3 *parsley*
4 *mint*
5 *thyme*
6 *chives*
7 *French tarragon*
8 *sage*

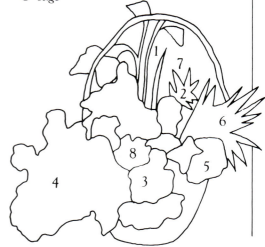

Appreciate the textures and fragrance of Mediterranean herbs in a basket near your door.

Tomato and Lettuce Window Box

As lettuce hearts develop in around ten days, you will find you can pick them, and replace them with smaller plants while waiting for the tomatoes to grow and ripen – around six to ten weeks, depending on the amount of light and warmth they receive.

Tomatoes are prone to aphids, and may need spraying occasionally. If they appear to be wilting, insure that they have enough water. You will need to pinch out trusses – wherever a new little stem grows directly between two stems – to prevent the plant from producing only tiny tomatoes.

Tumbler tomatoes will give a bushy trailing tomato that will break the line of the box, and does not need pinching out. Otherwise opt for Totem – a compact, upright variety that will not grow too tall.

For lettuce, romaine is useful as an upright variety for filling in between tomato plants; otherwise Little Gem would be good or even the red-tinged Lollo Rosso.

YOU WILL NEED

2 tomato plants, Tumbler or Totem
3 romaine lettuce
a window box around 2 feet long
rich potting compost
water-retaining gel pellets
(optional)
slow-release fertilizer granules
(optional)

54

1 Three lettuce and two tomato plants will give a good yield. Drill holes in the bottom of your window box if there are none already. Line the bottom with crockery or pebbles for drainage, then fill to the brim with rich potting compost.

2 You can add slow-release fertilizer and water-retaining gel pellets at this stage – scattered about halfway down. Remove the plants from their pots, teasing the roots out gently. Plant alternately, with lettuces at the sides and center.

3 Water well. Make sure the compost covers the roots well. Firm it down a little, and add more if necessary as it will sink with watering. Do not crowd the box with more plants because they require a lot of nutrients to produce a good crop.

QUICK TIPS

• Tomatoes need regular feeding and watering. Feed weekly with a liquid tomato fertilizer. Water twice daily in warm or windy weather. Spray to deter pests if necessary.
• Tumbler tomatoes are good for hanging baskets and boxes as they spill naturally over the sides and trail prettily. The tomatoes are also fairly small, sweet and juicy.
• Insure the root ball of the tomato plant is well below the compost level to prevent drying out. Water well.

Experiment with salad vegetables to produce a window box full of color and with edible results.

A Strawberry Basket

A strawberry basket will bring delicious results, and, with its white flowers and green foliage, will look attractive while you wait for it to bear fruit.

Ask the advice of your nursery or garden center when choosing plants. You are looking for varieties with smaller leaves than many grown in vegetable plots, which produce a large crop of fruit.

All standard strawberry plants have pretty white flowers before they are pollinated; some have variegated foliage. Those with pink flowers look particularly pretty, but some are not renowned for sweet-tasting fruit. Those used here, called *Fragaria* "Strawberries and Cream," are, however, delicious.

Early planting, say, in mid- to late spring, will give you a first strawberry crop in early summer, with another later in the season. To avoid frosts, you may wish to keep your basket in a greenhouse, but do keep the door open on warm days to let bees enter and pollinate the flowers, or else they will not produce fruit. An alternative is to wrap your basket in frost-proof fleece at night during the early part of the year. (This is available by the yard from many garden centers.) You will also find a few yards of this fleece invaluable for covering other baskets and boxes.

1 Line your basket with moss. Bringing the moss up and over the brim will hide the wire. Fill with rich compost until it is level with the top, and, if possible, add a season-long fertilizer. Check that this is suitable for fruit when you buy it.

2 Remove the plants from the pots, and tease the roots out to encourage them to take quickly. Arrange them at angles all around the basket when planting so that some will trail. If you can, plant some through the sides and bottom. Water well.

QUICK TIPS

● A strawberry basket needs a rich potting compost, regular feeding and a sunny position.
● Water when the compost is dry, but not too frequently as strawberries are particularly prone to mildew.
● Trim off any runners as the plant's energy will then be used to produce larger and sweeter fruit.
● Immediately after picking the fruit, cut off the leaves to about 3 inches above the crown.
● Look out for Perpetual (Remontant) varieties as these have a long fruiting season, beginning in early summer and then fruiting again in late summer. Other varieties may fruit only once a year.
● Guard against damage by squirrels and birds by covering with fine-mesh plastic net while the fruit is forming.
● Pick the ripe strawberries every few days. Do not remove them when still partially green or white – ripening produces natural sugars.

YOU WILL NEED

14-inch wire basket
5 strawberry plants
moss
rich potting compost

For delicate flowers, variegated foliage and sweet edible fruits, try planting a strawberry basket.

Country Cottage Window Box

Window boxes are particularly evocative of a rural idyll. For many of us, a cottage with roses around the door will remain a dream, but window boxes of fragrant lavender, stocks and chamomile are perfectly achievable.

A terracotta trough can be suitably aged by painting it with plain yogurt at the beginning of the season, and then letting nature's micro-organisms do their work and break down the yogurt to create an interesting "look."

Snow-in-summer and creeping jenny are plants known to many gardeners, but are not often used in window boxes and hanging baskets – their rampaging character will be contained by the box, and they are both fairly hardy, although they will not stand drying out. Monkey flower deserves a gold star for its longstanding versatility – flowering from late spring onward, it produces rewarding blooms and trails prettily.

YOU WILL NEED

a terracotta trough
broken crockery or pebbles
multi-purpose potting compost
3 stocks (*Matthiola*) · 1 snow-
in-summer (*Cerastium*)
1 dwarf lavender (*Lavandula*
"Hidcote") · 1 Swedish ivy
1 cream monkey flower
(*Mimulus*)
1 creeping jenny (*Lysimachia
nummularia aurea*)
1 chamomile (*Anthemis*)

1 Check that your window box has drainage holes. Cover these with a layer of crockery or pebbles. Add potting compost until it is level with the top of the box. Plan to have trailing plants to the front and taller plants to the rear.

2 Space the stocks out. Make sure the crown of the root is 1 inch below the surface. Add lavender and chamomile between the stocks, then, along the front, snow-in-summer, creeping jenny, Swedish ivy and mimulus.

QUICK TIPS

● Choose dwarf varieties of lavender, or it will grow too tall and block the light.
● Deadhead stocks, and they will bloom again.
● Age a terracotta window box by painting it with plain yogurt and leaving it on the ground outside for a few weeks.
● Choose more unusual trailing plants, such as mimulus and campanula, for a country look.

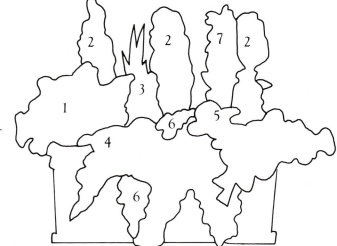

1 snow-in-summer
2 stocks
3 dwarf lavender
4 Swedish ivy
5 monkey flower
6 creeping jenny
7 chamomile

Use scented stocks, dwarf lavender and chamomile for a traditional combination of pastel colors.

Wild Flower Window Box

A window box of wild flowers makes an unusual contrast to bold displays of well-known plants. These European wild flowers are suitable for baskets and boxes.

Flowering from late spring to mid-summer
Yellow: rock rose, birdsfoot trefoil, horseshoe vetch, silverweed, monkey flower, feverfew
Blue: ivy-leaved toadflax, cornflower, heartsease, meadow cranesbill, bellflowers, wild thyme, wild marjoram
Pink/Red: herb Robert, pheasant's eye, poppy, mallow, cranesbill, columbine
White: barren strawberry
Flowering from late summer to mid-fall
Yellow: toadflax, creeping jenny
Blue: small scabious, bellflower, harebell
Flowering from late fall to mid-spring
Yellow: primrose, cowslip, tormentil
White: wild strawberry, sweet woodruff
Blue: heartsease, germander speedwell, forget-me-not, dog violet
Pink: scarlet pimpernel, herb Robert

1 Insure that the box has drainage holes, then cover the bottom with crockery or pebbles. Fill loosely with multi-purpose compost, adding fertilizer granules halfway. Water-retaining pellets are a good idea as many wild flowers thrive in damp conditions.

2 Start by planting the taller columbine to one end, with the cornflower at the other. Fill in with the mallow, feverfew and poppy, letting the flowering dead-nettle spill over the front of the box. Top with compost, and water well.

QUICK TIPS
• Wild flowers often thrive in semi-shady spots.
• Keep the compost moist; moisture-retaining gel is available and should be added when filling with compost.
• Provide adequate drainage by putting broken crockery or pebbles in the bottom.
• An asymmetrical arrangement can look particularly attractive. Plan your scheme to have larger plants at one end with perhaps a trailing plant at the other.
• Some garden centers have special wild flower areas – most plants are now clearly labeled, but it is worth making inquiries if you need to check the compatibility of certain plants.

YOU WILL NEED

water-retaining pellets or gel
1 columbine (*Aquilegia vulgaris*)
1 cornflower (*Centaura*)
1 dwarf mallow (*Malva*)
1 feverfew
(*Tanacetum parthenium*)
1 oriental poppy (*Papaver*)
1 spotted dead-nettle (*Lamium maculatum*)

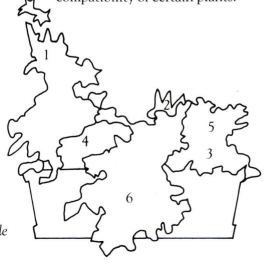

1 columbine
2 cornflower
3 dwarf mallow
4 feverfew
5 poppy
6 spotted dead-nettle

60

Create an asymmetrical arrangement using graceful columbine, dwarf mallow, feverfew and dead-nettle.

Wild Flower Hanging Basket

A wild flower garden need not necessarily be a rambling meadow. A wild flower basket can provide you with sturdy flowers you may recognize from the hedgerows of your childhood, with delicate blooms and fascinating foliage, all to be enjoyed as a compact sphere.

The one thing that could be a drawback with wild flowers is their brief flowering season, but this can be overcome by planting chronologically, so that at any one time some flowers are in bud while other blooms are fading. On page 60 we have listed wild flowers suitable for baskets and window boxes, and the seasons when they are in flower.

Your local garden center is likely to have a wild flower section, and you should be able to order other varieties through them. You should *never* take plants from the wild.

YOU WILL NEED

a 14-inch wire basket · moss
lightweight potting compost
a pot or bucket as a basket
holder
1 bellflower (*Campanula*)
1 pink wild geranium (dusky
cranesbill) (*Geranium*) · 1 blue
wild geranium (*Geranium*
"Johnson's Blue")
2 periwinkles (*Vinca*), one
variegated · 1 rock soapwort
(*Saponaria*) · 3 rock roses
(*Helianthemum*)

1 Having balanced the basket on a pot or bucket, line the basket with damp moss, greener side outermost. Place a liner of plastic, foam or fiber in the bottom, then fill with compost, adding slow-release fertilizer granules halfway.

2 Plant the cranesbill and rock roses in the center with the other plants at the sides. Guide these beneath the top wire to encourage them to trail down the sides, and cover the bottom of the basket. Fill the basket with compost and water well.

QUICK TIPS
● Find the wild flower corner of your local garden center, and study the plant labels.
● A wild flower leaflet is sometimes available too.
● Choose flowers which bloom in the same season where possible.
● Plan your color scheme ahead, or opt for a random assortment as here.
● Keep the basket well watered, and do not let the compost dry out.
● Never take plants from the wild.
● Thread some plants through the sides and bottom for a random ball arrangement.

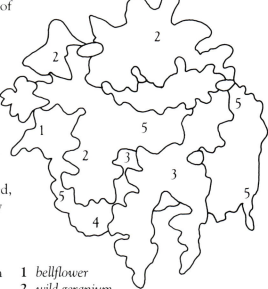

1 bellflower
2 wild geranium
3 periwinkle
4 rock soapwort
5 rock roses

Recreate the beauty of the countryside with a random mix of red and yellow rock roses, blue geraniums and periwinkle.

A Scented Window Box

Many plants with scented leaves need to be brushed past to release their perfume, but those with blooms often release their scent in the cool of the evening.

The tobacco plants used here will flower in sun or partial shade, and produce blooms from mid-summer until the early fall frosts. These varieties can grow up to 1 foot tall, which is tall enough for a window box, but they also tend to lean forward and trail prettily. Some varieties of tobacco plant grow even taller – so do check when buying.

The dwarf lavender prefers a sunny position, as does the scented geranium. These need to be planted in front of the tall tobacco plants where their foliage and scent will mingle.

One scented plant not used here is the lily. Dwarf varieties are now available.

Some window boxes, such as this one, are attached to the wall, and will need to be planted in situ. Others have a plastic liner, which means that you can plant on a suitable surface and then slide the liner into the window box.

1 Check that your window box has drainage holes. You may need to drill some. Line the box with slit plastic and crockery for drainage. Fill with a multi-purpose compost, and plan your planting scheme before you plant the box.

2 At this stage you could scatter some slow-release fertilizer about halfway down the box. Plant the large scented geranium so that it will trail over the front of the box. Then fill in with the lavender, and plant the taller tobacco plants to the rear.

QUICK TIPS

- Choose dwarf varieties of lavender and tobacco plants as some are fairly tall.
- Check that the tobacco plants you have chosen are fragrant – some varieties are more heavily scented than others.
- You can buy liners for wall-mounted window boxes which make planting far easier.
- Place your box where it will be brushed by people passing by; otherwise the scent will be released in only small quantities.
- Lavender and scented geraniums prefer a sunny site.

1 *white tobacco plants*
2 *mixed tobacco plants*
3 *lavender*
4 *lemon-scented geranium*

Combine color and fragrance with red and white tobacco plants, dwarf lavender and lemon-scented geranium.

A Scented Basket

Hang a scented basket where you will brush against the leaves as you walk by, releasing their fragrance. Most helichrysum have no scent, but this tiny-leafed version releases a wonderful aroma when you rub it between your fingers. Hanging baskets of this silvery plant alone can look most effective.

Pineapple mint, like all mint, can be invasive when planted in a container, but it is worth including for its pleasant fruity fragrance when the leaves are gently crushed – hence its name. To make sure the mint does not spread too far, you can contain root growth by pushing in vertical sections of slate when planting, or simply keeping it in its pot.

Pinks (*Dianthus*) and heliotrope look good together, and have a delicate perfume. The pansies are included not for their scent but to complement the color scheme.

Pinks grow happily on poor soils, and dislike soil that is rich or very acidic. If you have very chalky garden soil, you could mix a little of this, or slaked garden lime, into multi-purpose compost.

YOU WILL NEED

1 tray of pinks (8 *Dianthus* × *allwoodii* "Doris") · 1 pineapple mint (*Mentha*) · 1 *Helichrysum microphylla* · 1 heliotrope 1 pot white pansies (*Viola hederacea*) · plastic for lining · hand-operated or electric drill · multi-purpose compost · wood preservative

1 If your basket is wooden, you will need to drill holes in the bottom first. Wood preservative will prevent it from rotting. Let it dry for a day, then line it with slit plastic. Cover the bottom with pebbles, and fill with mixed compost.

2 Start by planting the pinks centrally within the basket. Then add the heliotrope, helichrysum, pineapple mint and pansies in each of the four corners. Top with compost, then water. Hang in a sunny position, and deadhead regularly.

QUICK TIPS

● Prepare a wooden basket by drilling holes for drainage.
● Use a wood preservative to prolong the life of your basket.
● Line it with plastic to protect the wood.
● Cut slits for drainage.
● Pinks need full sun in order to flower, so you may need to move your basket to a sunny spot.
● Helichrysum needs to be kept moist, so daily watering is important.

● Stop the mint from spreading by keeping it within its pot or cornering it with slates.
● Add slaked lime to multi-purpose compost for pinks, which dislike an acid soil.

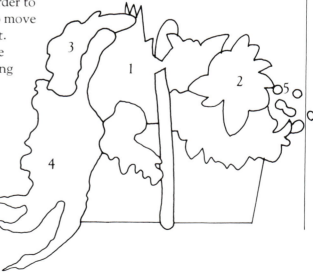

1 pinks
2 pineapple mint
3 heliotrope
4 helichrysum
5 pansies

Pinks and heliotrope, offset by pineapple mint and helichrysum, will give a soft pastel scheme with a lingering fragrance.

A Window Box for a Shady Area

Bring light into a shady spot with a window box of flowers and foliage.

Few of us would plan a window box for shade without being prompted, but it can be particularly rewarding. You may not have a box overflowing with flowers, but many shade-loving plants have graceful lines, strong colors and textures that work well together.

Some plants do flower in shade, of course. You could use impatiens or fuchsias. We chose to use bedding begonias, which flower in partial shade, for their lustrous dark leaves. The hardy dead-nettle is also surprisingly attractive, and can be found with yellow or pink blossoms.

Shade-loving plants appreciate moist conditions, so it is worth including moisture-retaining gel when planting.

YOU WILL NEED

two-foot wooden window box
wood preservative · plastic or other liner · crockery or pebbles
multi-purpose compost
water-retaining gel
1 nephrolepis or Boston fern
(*Nephrolepis exaltata* "Bostoniensis") · 2 hostas
(*H. fortunei* "Aureamarginata")
1 yellow dead-nettle (*Lamium galeobdolon* "Herman's Pride") · 1 *Fuchsia* "Autumnale" · 3 bedding begonia (*Begonia semperflorens*)

1 Treat wooden boxes with wood preservative, and let air for a day. Check that there are drainage holes, and drill some if there are not. Line the bottom with crockery or pebbles, and fill to halfway up the box with multi-purpose compost.

2 Add water-retaining pellets and slow-release fertilizer granules at the halfway stage. While they are still in their pots, plan your planting scheme; i.e., where you would like trailing foliage, height and color. Move them about until you are happy.

3 Start with the largest plant – in this case the fern – then plant the dead-nettle at the other end of the box. Fill in with hostas and begonias, with fuchsia trailing over the front. **Tip**: snip off browning fronds or leaves.

1 Boston fern
2 hosta
3 dead-nettle
4 Fuchsia "Autumnale"
5 bedding begonia

Textured ferns and variegated cream and green hostas contrast well with bright begonias in a coral container.

A Hanging Basket for a Shady Spot

Shady corners should not be forgotten. Warm planting schemes like these shades of peach are quite in order.

The sunny border in your garden is frequently the most colorful, and the shadiest spot often a problem area. Most hanging baskets thrive in sun, but many plants also bloom well in semi-shade.

Fuchsias, in particular, are known for their partiality to shade, and impatiens, too, will flower without sunshine provided they are placed in the shade only after the first flowers have opened.

Some gardeners are surprised to learn that begonias will flower in partial shade. Pansies are known as winter-flowering plants, so it is not unusual for them to bloom in a shady corner.

The alternative is to choose plants that have particularly attractive foliage – ferns and hostas are an obvious choice. These need damp soil and moist conditions, so frequent spraying and a water-retaining agent are important.

YOU WILL NEED

a 14-inch basket · moss
multi-purpose compost
plastic or other liner
1 coral begonia (*Begonia* "Chanson")
1 *Convolvulus mauritanicus*
1 semi-trailing fuchsia (*F.* "Orange Crystal")
1 monkey flower (*Mimulus*)
2 impatiens

1 Gather your ingredients. Place the basket over a bucket to prevent it from rocking, then line it with damp moss, green side outermost. Line it with plastic, then fill it with compost, including water-retaining and slow-release fertilizer granules.

2 Plant the fuchsia, impatiens and monkey flower on three sides of the basket with the upright begonia in the center. Arrange the convolvulus to trail beneath the top wire. Plant one impatiens through the sides. Water well.

QUICK TIPS

● Avoid splashing water on the leaves of the begonia as this can cause rotting.

● Shade-loving plants generally appreciate lots of water, so keep the compost moist. Fuchsias and begonias both need plenty of water.

● Take a closer look at the strongly defined foliage plants, including most ferns. They can look surprisingly attractive, particularly if your window box is painted a bold color (see page 38).

● Many winter-flowering plants, such as pansies, will flower in shady spots.

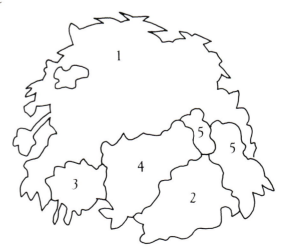

1 *coral begonia*
2 *convolvulus*
3 *semi-trailing fuchsia*
4 *monkey flower*
5 *impatiens*

Choose deep peach and blues for an unusual color combination of flowers for a shady spot.

An Alpine Window Box

The small size and delicate appearance of alpines often belie their hardiness. Used to surviving in mountainous regions, they can withstand dry periods, but dislike being overwatered.

You will need a mix of fine horticultural gravel and compost to provide a well-drained soil. A thick layer of gravel or crockery on the bottom of the box is also important. Terracotta is a particularly suitable material for an alpine window box as any excess moisture will drain away naturally through the porous walls and bottom of the box. (You will still need drainage holes, of course.) Plan your display by placing the plants in their pots within the window box. Try to mix flowering and foliage plants and to group complementary colors together.

You may well feel tempted by other alpines when faced with a display at your garden center or nursery. Whatever you choose, it is worth including the alpine favorites: sedums and saxifrage, houseleeks, lewisia and rock roses.

1 Start by mixing the gravel and compost in roughly 50/50 proportions. Then line the bottom of the window box with a substantial layer of broken clay pots or pebbles. The rooting system of alpines is very shallow, so they will not need deep compost.

2 Tap, rather than twist, the plants from their pots, then gently tease out the root system before planting. Starting at one end, work along the box, planting one plant to the front and the next to the rear; a large stone in the middle looks effective.

3 Water carefully, avoiding the crowns of the plants and the tops of leaves as alpines do not like to be waterlogged. If there are spaces to fill, you can add other suitable plants later on. Look in the alpine section of your garden center.

YOU WILL NEED

fine horticultural gravel
multi-purpose compost
creeping jenny
(*Lysimachia nummularia*)
thrift (*Armeria maritima*
"Dusseldorf Pride")
houseleek (*Sempervivum*
"Wolcott")
Campanula carpatica
1 *Chrysanthemum hosmariense*
1 *Silene schafta* "Robusta"

1 *creeping jenny*
2 *thrift*
3 *houseleek*
4 *campanula*
5 *chrysanthemum*
6 *silene*

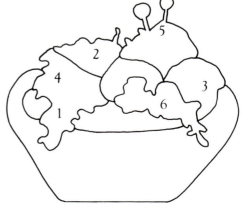

Make the most of delicate alpine flowers with an eye-level container. Pink thrift and blue dwarf bellflower will spread and intermingle.   73

An Alpine Hanging Basket

Alpines prefer a sunny situation and dryish soil, so water sparingly. If you have a particularly rainy week, it is worth sheltering the plants under cover for a while. Alpines hate having wet roots, so you must make sure that the drainage is good. Mix the compost 50/50 with horticultural gravel to give a free-draining mixture. We used a thin fiber liner through which moisture can pass. It has slits to enable planting at lower levels so that plants can cover the bottom of the basket.

This basket was planted in early spring when most of the plants were very small and relatively inexpensive. It is composed of plants which will flower in groups from early spring to late summer and early fall. Hung from a post of climbing clematis, it creates a pretty corner beside a doorway.

1 Gather your ingredients. Plan to have trailing plants at the sides and the more upright sisyrinchium, rock rose and pink in the center. Begin by inserting the liner and mixture of gravel and compost. Then plant the rock rose and pink.

2 Plant the geraniums and gypsophila in clumps to form larger plants later. Encircle the pink with trailing plants, planting from below and through the slits in the liner wherever possible. Water gently, and place in a sunny spot.

YOU WILL NEED

fine horticultural gravel
multi-purpose compost
3 *Gypsophila repens* "Dubia"
1 *Veronica pectinata*
1 tumbling ted (*Saponaria ocymoides*)
1 *Campanula* "Birch Hybrid"
3 *Geranium sanguineum striatum*
1 *Sedum spurium* "Album"
1 *Sedum spurium* "Purple Carpet"
1 *Diascia* "Ruby Field"
1 *Sisyrinchium* "Mrs. Spivey"
1 pink (*Dianthus* "Dewdrop")
1 rock rose
(*Helianthemum* "The Bride")

QUICK TIPS

● Alpines like well-drained soil, so mix half horticultural gravel and half multi-purpose compost in a bucket before starting to fill your basket.
● Many alpines dislike having the top of their root ball (the crown) watered. Aim to water between plants where possible.
● Make slits in fiber liners for planting through the sides and bottom to insure an evenly covered hanging basket.
● Choose plants that flower in succession whenever possible.

1 Gypsophila repens
2 *veronica*
3 *tumbling ted*
4 *campanula*
5 *geranium*
6 *sedum*
7 *diascia*
8 *sisyrinchium*
9 *pink*
10 *rock rose*

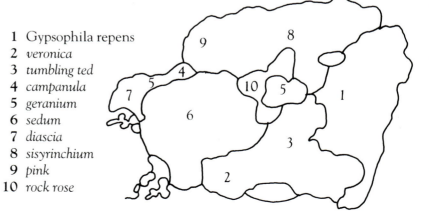

For alpine flowers all year round, this combination includes gypsophila, pinks, tumbling ted and sedums.

FALL PLANTS

All too often, as mid-fall approaches and our bright summer baskets die off, gardeners empty their hanging baskets and window boxes, and put them away until the following spring.

The fall and winter months are just the time when your house and garden need extra life and color, and this can be very easily achieved simply by clearing dead foliage and adding hardier plants which can withstand colder, less sunny conditions and still give a good display of gentle color and texture.

Fall Window Box

Instead of the usual gold and yellow colors of fall which, incidentally, can be achieved with a mix of miniature chrysanthemums, we have opted for a more delicate silver gray and pink scheme. Planted in mid-fall, it will still be looking healthy in early spring, by which time the plants will have intermingled charmingly.

1 After insuring that there are drainage holes, line the bottom of the box with broken crockery or pebbles. Half-fill the window box with ericaceous (acidic) soil. Test your planting plan. Aim to have larger plants to the rear.

2 Hebes grow fairly tall – up to 30 inches. When you are happy with your plan, firm the largest plants in first. Then fill in with the heathers and ornamental cabbage along the front, alternating pink and white as we have done in our arrangement.

QUICK TIPS
● Use ericaceous (lime-free) compost for hebes and heathers – you can buy this already prepared in bags, or mix your own using multi-purpose potting compost and a powder.
● Only use hebes if you have a fairly tall window. Window boxes can be used to give you extra privacy if the planting arrangement is tall.
● Heathers like a rich, moist compost, so keep the arrangement well watered, and this window box will survive for years.

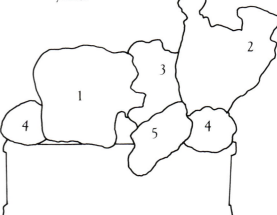

1 Hebe *"Kirkii"*
2 Hebe *"Seduisante"*
3 *artemisia*
4 *heathers*
5 *ornamental cabbage*

For a fall scheme of pink, white and silver gray, opt for hebes and heathers filled in with ornamental cabbages.

FALL HANGING BASKET

A Pansy Ball

One of the most reliable flowers for fall and winter baskets has to be the pansy, but rather than the usual half hanging basket, you could try a pansy ball.

It is possible to wire together two regular half-baskets, or you can now buy basket balls which clip together. If making your own, try to choose smaller baskets because, when filled with soil and water, they are very heavy indeed.

You can buy a tray of bedding plants in mid-spring. These are easy to insert from the outside. If using a wire basket, you will need to line it with moss and polyethylene.

To make planting easier, you could balance each half on a filled flowerpot.

Let the baskets settle for a few days before joining, or overfill one half. Otherwise, there will be insufficient compost and moisture around the plants in the top section of the ball.

YOU WILL NEED

tray of 48 bedding pansies (*Viola* "Padparadja Forerunner Tangerine")
moss-polyethylene liner
multi-purpose potting compost
2 hanging baskets, 14 inches in diameter

1 Start by making holes at regular intervals around the bottom of the first half. Insert the plants from the outside, roots first. Wrap the roots in a small cone of polyethylene to prevent them from being damaged. Add layers of compost as you work upward.

2 Before joining, water to let the compost settle. Overfill one half of the basket, and cover it with plastic. Invert it over the second basket, and slide the plastic out. If it is not a clip-together version, wire the two halves together.

QUICK TIPS

● Overfill both baskets so that, when placed together, the compost is compact, and there are no airpockets where plant roots could dry out.

● Wrap plant roots in a cone of plastic (rather than damp newspaper) as this will slide through more easily.

● A small, empty flowerpot buried in the top half will make watering easier. If this pot will be visible when the ball is hung up, you can drop in a potted-up pansy, and then simply remove it for watering.

● If you have a plastic, clip-together ball, you can plant a pansy ball later in the season, using full-size plants. To make the gaps large enough to insert the pansy root from the outside in, clip away the vertical or horizontal plastic struts.

To maintain the strength of the ball, insure that these enlarged gaps are not made directly beside each other.

● Remove the chains while filling in with pansies, but remember their positions while planting.

A ball of fall pansies of this unusual orange-red variety will bring color through the winter months.

EVERGREEN PLANTS

Although many of us opt for evergreens, such as ivy, somewhere in our spring and summer baskets, it is rare to see an evergreen basket bringing life to a doorway through the winter months. However, the bright-berried plants and tiny flowered evergreens, with their glossy and red or gold-tinged foliage, will last through some of the coldest weather, and can bring a great deal of pleasure.

Most evergreens are far hardier than summer bedding plants, and are unlikely to suffer from drying out through the damp winter months, as watering once a week or so will be enough unless the weather is particularly mild and windy.

An Evergreen Hanging Basket

Evergreens merit greater use than only in winter or as backdrop foliage; they are also extremely useful in baskets hung in shady spots – box, elaeagnus, periwinkle, creeping fig and ferns are all successful in deep or semi-shade.

YOU WILL NEED

moss · plastic liner
multi-purpose compost
1 *Cotoneaster salicifolius*
"Autumn Fire"
1 *Cotoneaster dammeri*
1 periwinkle (*Vinca major variegata*)

1 Collect your ingredients. You will need moss and a plastic liner to help to hold water. Some slits in the plastic will be necessary for drainage. Remove the chains, if possible, to make planting easier. Line the basket with moss, greener side outermost.

2 Line the moss with plastic liner, and fill with compost. Set the more upright cotoneaster to the rear and the periwinkle trailing over and through the sides. Add compost and water well. Feed after a few months have passed.

QUICK TIPS

● Use versatile evergreens as a foliage backdrop to year-round planting, for winter schemes and in shady spots.
● Water weekly. If evergreen plants in a hanging basket appear to be drying out, immerse in a bucket of water until bubbles stop rising. The root ball is now moist. Rehang and water every few weeks throughout the winter months.

● Aim to cover the bottom of the basket by encouraging plants to trail through the sides.
● Terracotta and glazed ceramic containers can crack in winter – so you may need to move them in hard frosts. Some, of course, are frost-proof.

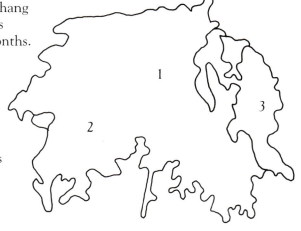

1 Cotoneaster salicifolius
2 Cotoneaster dammeri
3 *periwinkle*

The glossy leaves and red berries of cotoneaster intermingle with variegated periwinkle in a midwinter basket.

An Evergreen Window Box

At a time when most garden plants have died back and lost their color and leaves, you can still bring cheer to the dull winter months with lustrous skimmias, red-tinged leucothoe and feathery juniper.

Leaf color and texture are part of the joy of winter gardening, although evergreen plants will give color and strength to a display all year round. When winter is over, you can add spring and summer flowers to contrast with the glossy foliage.

You might think these shrubs would grow too large for window boxes and hanging baskets, but all plants adapt their size to suit the container they live in, and are restrained in their growth and spread by the size of their root ball.

The glossy green leaves and purple sprouting of the skimmia will look good beside the colorful red leaves of the leucothoe. The spreading juniper gives contrasting shape and texture to the arrangement.

YOU WILL NEED

plastic liner for the box
multi-purpose compost
2 *Skimmia japonica* "Rubella"
1 *Juniperus sabina*
"Tamariscifolia" (spreading fir)
1 *Leucothoe axillaris* "Scarletta"
1 *Gaultheria procumbens*
(berried)

1 First plan your arrangement with the plants still in their pots. Consider the shape of the spreading fir and the location of your window box in relation to shrubs below, or climbers growing around your window.

2 It is often safer to plant boxes in situ, or to fill a plastic liner. Having half-filled your box with multi-purpose compost, fill in with the largest plants first and finally the berried gaultheria. Lastly, add compost to just below the top edge of the box.

QUICK TIPS
● Choose a group of plants with foliage that is varied in both color and texture.
● Plan for one plant to trail over and break the line of the box.
● With heavy stone or composite boxes, either plant in situ, or fill a plastic liner separately then slot it in.
● Larger plants will be restrained by the space allowed to the root ball, and so will not grow excessively large.

1 Skimmia japonica
2 *juniper*
3 *leucothoe*
4 *gaultheria*

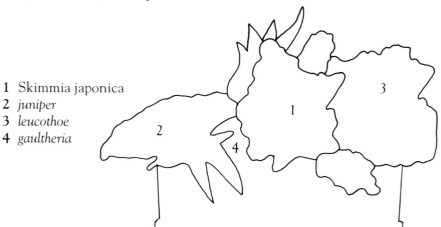

Accentuate the glowing foliage of leucothoe by mixing it with the glossy leaves of skimmias and gaultheria and feathery fronds of juniper.   83

CHRISTMAS FOLIAGE

From the gold-tinged leaves of variegated holly to the luminous white of cyclamen and glossy, berried evergreens, Christmas offers an opportunity for some delightful displays.

A Christmas Hanging Basket

You may never have thought of making a hanging basket specifically for the Christmas season, but among all the artificial tinsel and glitz it will seem refreshingly delicate and natural.

Roses can last for two weeks or longer if given vials of water of the type usually provided for orchids. These can be wired and hidden among the greenery.

Red ribbons make decorative hangings, and the cyclamen will survive happily in a sheltered porch while temperatures are at freezing or just above.

YOU WILL NEED

multi-purpose compost/plastic
woven twig basket and wreath
13 inches in diameter
1 yard 2½-inch-wide red/gold,
wired Ribbon
3½ yards 1-inch-wide red
ribbon
8 plastic vials
1 cyclamen · 8 white roses
4 small ivies (*Hedera*)
1 stem of eucalyptus,
snowberries (*Symphoricarpos*)

1 Collect the ingredients. Line the basket with slit plastic, and start by filling it with the cyclamen sitting upright in the center and the ivies trailing over the sides. Top with lightweight multi-purpose compost. Water carefully.

2 Cut the rose stems to 8 inches, and thread them through the wreath into vials of water. Thread the larger green stems around the wreath first, finishing with the more delicate ruscus and snow-berries, and also inserting these into the vials.

QUICK TIPS

● Small plastic vials of the type available from florists, and generally used for orchids and corsages, will give an arrangement such as this a lifespan of around two weeks.

● If a frost is forecast, bring the arrangement into a cool hallway for the night.

● Use wire-edged ribbon for impressive bows – it is easier to tie and far less floppy.

● If you wish for a more permanent Christmas basket without vials of water, simply combine cyclamen and ivy in a container, and hang it up on red ribbons.

1 *roses*
2 *cyclamen*
3 *eucalyptus*
4 *snowberry*
5 *ivy*

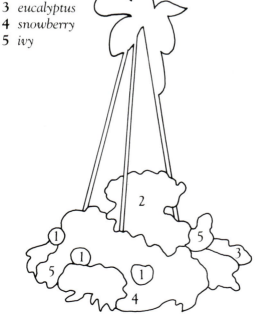

Tie the narrow ribbons onto the outer wicker wreath to form a balanced arrangement when held from the top, and tie the wreath to a cup-hook, or something similar, secured into a wooden porch frame. Tie the wired ribbon into a large bow, and pin it on to hide the top fastenings.

A festive red and white combination of roses and cyclamen wound about a rustic wreath with ivy and snowberries.

A Christmas Window Box with a Tree

Add to the seasonal festivities with a tree-filled window box full of Christmas charm.

Dramatic red berries, glossy green leaves and symmetrical fir trees, enhanced by the mellow warmth of a teak window box, make a Christmas arrangement that is both traditional and yet satisfyingly unfamiliar, so that it will catch the attention of visitors.

For too many of us, outside Christmas decorations are limited to fairy lights and a door wreath, when, in fact, there is a wealth of plants in the garden center with leaves that have an interesting shape or texture, or bear bright berries, just waiting to be grouped in seasonal harmony.

This arrangement will last from mid-fall until spring with little care needed, apart from a weekly watering. If you wish, you could add various extra decorations, such as silver or gold chains of stars, for the Christmas week, but this balance of Christmas color has a subtle charm of its own that really needs no extra adornment.

YOU WILL NEED

plastic liner for box
ericaceous compost
2 *Skimmia reevesiana*
3 ivies (*Hedera*)
4 small upright conifers

1 Gather together your ingredients. Start by making holes in the plastic liner of the box, then add a small layer of gravel or crockery to aid drainage. Half-fill the box with ericaceous compost (for acid-loving plants) to maintain healthy growth.

2 Firm in the two largest plants (the skimmias), leaning their berried leaves toward the front where possible. Follow this by planting the four upright conifers to the rear. Fill in at each end and along the front with the ivies to soften the edges.

QUICK TIPS

● Use berried plants other than holly in Christmas baskets to create an arrangement that is slightly unusual.

● Water weekly when the Christmas season is over, and this window box is likely to last for at least a year or even longer.

● Despite being hardwood, teak window boxes benefit from a treatment of wood preservative to keep them looking warm and mellow. An alternative is to use a plastic liner.

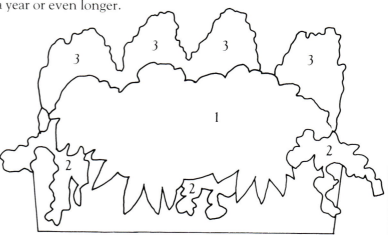

1 *skimmia*
2 *ivy*
3 *conifers*

Four miniature conifers and glossy-berried skimmias create a refreshingly natural display for Christmas.

A Christmas Basket as an Indoor Arrangement

For a more unusual Christmas color scheme, we decided to opt for gold and green, bringing indoors plants that are often banished to the garden.

This arrangement could be used on a deep windowsill, or even in a large fireplace if watered regularly. The plants could be moved to the garden after Christmas if you wish. A few days before you plant the basket, stain it in your chosen color. We decided on spruce green in order not to detract from the color scheme, and yet still be in keeping with a Christmas theme. Let it dry thoroughly for a few days, then line it with plastic. If you make drainage holes, you will need to water the basket outside; otherwise careful watering is essential in order to avoid waterlogging.

YOU WILL NEED

ericaceous potting compost
a large garden basket
dark green woodstain
large candle · narrow gold ribbon
1 yard gold cord
a gold cherub and 3 gold baubles
florist's wire · 5 dried quince
osmanthus (*Osmanthus heterophyllus* "Tricolor")
yellow fir (*Thuja orientalis*)
spotted laurel (*Aucuba japonica*)
Euonymus fortunei
Euphorbia · 4 ivies

1 Half-fill the basket with a lightweight ericaceous compost as the osmanthus, in particular, is an acid-loving plant. Start by firming in the largest plants (the *Thuja* and spotted laurel), twisting the pots gently to remove the root ball intact.

2 Bear in mind where the basket will sit, so you can position smaller plants to the front. When the larger plants are in, you can wind the narrow gold ribbon around the candle, and choose a place for it where its flame cannot burn the basket handle.

3 Place the candle firmly in position, so that it cannot fall over. Add the smaller ivy, and, when the basket is in place, arrange the quince both inside and out. Finally, wind the thicker gold cord around the handle, using wire for the cherub and baubles.

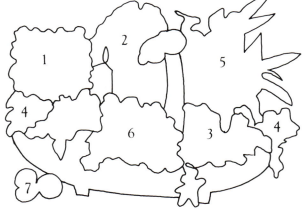

1 osmanthus
2 Thuja orientalis
3 euonymus
4 ivy
5 spotted laurel
6 euphorbia
7 quince

88

The harmonious tones of thuja and holly combine with spotted laurel and shiny baubles to make a basket of rich greens and golds.

CHILDREN'S BASKETS AND BOXES

It is not always possible to find a suitable space for your children to garden, nor to keep a child's garden contained within a set area. This is where baskets and window boxes prove rewarding.

Choose bright colors and easy-to-grow plants that are not likely to disappoint. Petunias and marigolds are an obvious choice, as are impatiens and lobelia.

Results from window boxes and hanging baskets are relatively speedy. Rather than growing from seed, use plants of a reasonable size so that growing time is reasonably short.

A Hanging Basket for Children

Children will enjoy planting baskets. To them, daily watering is not a chore but a pleasure, although you will have to check that watering is carried out regularly and not overenthusiastically! A simple basket could be the start of an interest in gardening for years to come.

> ### YOU WILL NEED
> a wire basket
> moss · plastic liner
> multi-purpose potting compost
> 2 *Petunia* "Red Stripe"
> 6 impatiens
> 2 *Verbena* "Red Cascade"
> 1 helichrysum

1 Let the children line the basket with moss, greener side outermost. Line it with slit plastic. Half-fill the basket with compost, and plant the petunias in the top. An attractive alternative would be a trailing petunia hybrid.

2 With some adult help, plant the impatiens at intervals through the sides of the basket, so that they will eventually almost cover the bottom. The verbena and helichrysum can be planted below the top of the basket, so that they will trail.

3 After planting, top with compost and water well. It is worth giving the children the responsibility of daily watering and deadheading blooms, so that they can appreciate the results of their first attempt and may try other arrangements.

1 *petunia*
2 *impatiens*
3 *verbena*
4 *helichrysum*

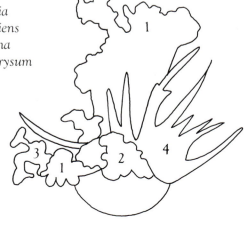

90

Red-and-white-striped petunias, cascading verbena and white impatiens will meet most children's desire for bright simplicity.

Children's Window Boxes

Yellow marigolds and orange nasturtiums seem made for children as they are easy-to-grow summer annuals that make a splash of color.

Children like to be part of every stage in gardening, from selecting plants (you will need to guide them toward compact, bushy plants) to planting and watering.

If you discuss the heights to which the plants will grow, the children will see the logic of planting them in descending order, with the trailing plants at the front. This is the ideal opportunity for a botany lesson – how root systems work, how plants use chlorophyll to turn sunlight into food.

We used a number of plants in order to give an impressive display – many more, and the amount of soil and water the basket can hold would not support them. Should you notice any pending disasters, you can do a little surreptitious gardening or replacement after the gardeners have gone to bed, to avoid unnecessary disappointment.

1 Make drainage holes in the bottom of the window box if there are none. Add a few handfuls of gravel for drainage, then half-fill with multi-purpose compost and some slow-release fertilizer and water-retaining granules (optional).

2 Plant the golden marguerites and snapdragons to the rear, with the French marigolds and nasturtiums in the center and lobelia at the front. Arrange the felicia to trail over one side. Top with compost. Firm in the plants, and water well.

QUICK TIPS

• Let the children choose the colors of plants for themselves if possible. Bright colors are likely to be most popular.
• Choose fairly reliable plants, such as marigolds, lobelia and petunias, and aim to keep an eye on them yourself.
• Let the children plant the basket or window box, and take care of it by watering and deadheading.
• Small baskets tend to dry out very quickly, so are not a good idea.
• Be very careful that any plants you use are not poisonous.

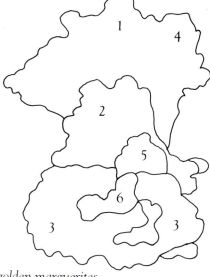

1 golden marguerites
2 French marigolds
3 lobelia
4 snapdragons
5 felicia
6 nasturtiums

Choose the flowers of childhood – snapdragons, daisies, marigolds and nasturtiums – for a basket that brims with life and color.

BUDGET IDEAS:
A Budget Hanging Basket

It is easy to buy plants in season and create impressive window boxes and baskets in the space of an hour, but this can prove expensive. Many plants can be grown from seed or cuttings, and others bought to fill in, if necessary, when your basket or box is ready to be planted.

Fuchsias, geraniums, *Petunia* "Surfinia," and impatiens are all easy to grow from cuttings. You can simply stand the cutting in a glass of water for a couple of weeks until several white roots have grown. The more professional method, however, is to cut the stem straight across, dip it in hormone rooting powder and insert it in a seeding potting compost that is 50 percent sharp sand and 50 percent peat.

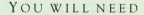

1 Sow the seed thinly in trays of fine potting compost in early spring. Water with a fine spray. Cover with plastic wrap, and keep in a warm place until the first leaves appear. Remove the cover. Transplant the seedlings at around 2 inches tall.

2 The fuchsia, "Surfinia" and impatiens can be grown from cuttings. We lined our basket with foam, which is a good water retainer and can be hidden by plants. Plant the fuchsia in the center, angling the other plants to trail through.

QUICK TIPS
- Use a saucer and knife to help to control the position of the seeds on the compost.
- Cover the seeds with plastic wrap with holes pierced in it to prevent too much condensation. When the first leaves appear, lift the plastic wrap each day to "air" the plants.
- Leave the seed tray in a warm, light but not too bright place to let the seeds germinate. If it seems very bright, lay a sheet of newspaper over the tray.
- When transplanting, hold the seedlings by their top leaves not by the roots. Use a pencil to make holes in the compost.

1 *lobelia*
2 *impatiens*
3 *fuchsia*
4 Petunia "Surfinia"
5 *verbena*
6 Bidens aurea

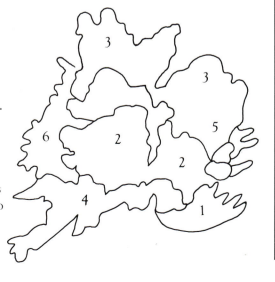

Create a basket brimming with color from seeds and cuttings. Fuchsias, "Surfinia," verbena and *Bidens aurea* are prolific.

A Budget Window Box

You can achieve a spectacular window box with a very low financial outlay. Most of these plants were grown from cuttings, and the trailing lobelia and verbena from seed. Growing from seed is easier if you have a greenhouse, but seeds and cuttings will also grow happily on a warm windowsill.

Start the seeds off in a tray of moist compost placed in a warm place for ten days or so. Cover the tray with plastic wrap with tiny holes in it. If necessary, use a sheet of newspaper to keep out very bright light. Ready-made window box gardening kits are now available with narrow seed boxes and raised, clear-plastic lids with air holes. When the seeds have germinated and the first leaves appear, take off the cover, and move the tray to a sunny position.

YOU WILL NEED

1 packet lobelia seeds
1 packet verbena seeds
1 packet white
daisy (*Bellis*) seeds
1 pendulous begonia
1 bedding begonia
5 impatiens (*Impatiens walleriana*)
2 zonal geraniums
(*Pelargonium × hortorum*)
a seed tray
multi-purpose compost
crockery or gravel
season-long fertilizer
water-retaining granules
(optional)

1 Sow the lobelia and verbena in early spring, transplanting the seedlings a month later. Take cuttings of other plants before the first frosts arrive, planting them in pots after four weeks or so. Feed the compost weekly with liquid fertilizer.

2 Plant your window box at the end of spring. Fill with a layer of crockery, then multi-purpose compost. Plant the geraniums, impatiens and begonias, then fill in with trailing plants.

QUICK TIPS

● Mix tiny seeds with very dry sand to make fine planting easier.
● Cover germinating seeds with plastic wrap to keep the compost moist, or newspaper to keep out very bright light.
● Root cuttings in a mixture of 50 percent peat and 50 percent coarse sand.

● If seedlings start to become too leggy in their search for light, build up soil around the stem, and move them somewhere a little cooler.
● Make a note of planting times and how your seeds progress, for reference in future years.

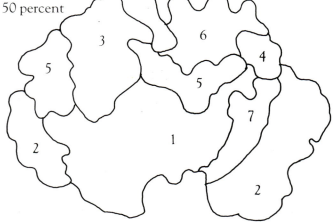

1 lobelia
2 verbena
3 pendulous begonia
4 bedding begonia
5 impatiens
6 geraniums
7 white daisies

A window box in shades of blue, pink and purple can cost very little when grown from seeds and cuttings.

How to Hang a Basket

Choosing a site

A spot that receives both sun and shade is best. Avoid north- and south-facing walls if possible, as these are often too shady or too hot. A drafty corner is also best avoided.

A number of plants will thrive in shady areas. Take a look at our displays on pages 68–71. Shade-loving plants for summer include begonias, bellflowers, creeping fig, ferns, fuchsia, honeysuckle, hosta, jasmine, monkey flower, pansy, impatiens, philodendron, pick-a-back plant and tobacco plants. In spring, bulbs such as lily of the valley, daffodils, tulips and snake's head fritillary will flower happily in semi-shade. Other spring-flowering plants which enjoy partially shaded sites include periwinkle, primrose, violets and azaleas.

Brackets

Wrought iron is the strongest and most suitable material. Choose a size to suit the diameter of your basket, and to allow some space between it and the wall to prevent the basket from damaging the plants.

Basket size	Bracket size
10 inches	9 inches
12 inches	9 inches
14 inches	9 inches
16 inches	12 inches
18 inches	12 inches
20 inches	14 inches
24 inches	16 inches
30 inches	18 inches

The bracket will have to cope with a heavy load, so secure it properly with screws and wall anchors of the correct gauge and length. Check for tightness from time to time throughout the year.

YOU WILL NEED

electric drill with correct size drill bit for screws
extension cord
screws – 2 inches long
wall anchors of the same length, regular or hollow-wall depending on surface, i.e., brick or stucco
colored crayon · measuring tape
straight or crosshead screwdriver

Practical tips

Installing a bracket is very similar to putting up a shelf bracket. Baskets are very heavy when full and being watered, and will need sturdy fasteners. Some brackets come with the correct length screw and wall anchor. If you are attaching to stucco, a hollow wall anchor, which splays out when inserted, is a good choice.

First insure that the surface your bracket will rest on is relatively smooth. The top screw will be taking most of the strain, so insure that this will be secured into a solid surface, i.e., brick rather than mortar.

Imagine the height that your basket will fall to when hung by the chains. Do

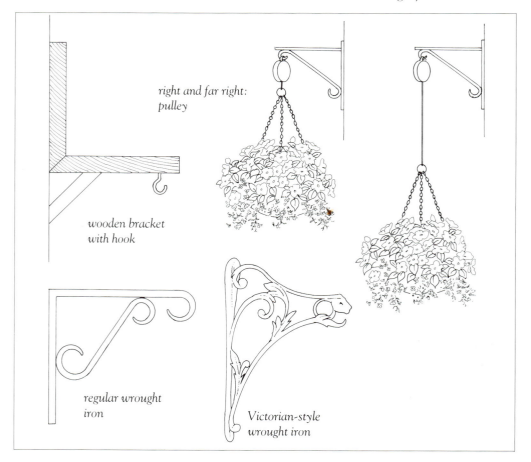

right and far right: pulley

wooden bracket with hook

regular wrought iron

Victorian-style wrought iron

not make it too high as you do not want to see only the underside of the basket. However, you also need to take into account whether it will be in the way of anyone walking by, and if it is likely to be a danger. A heavy basket can cause an unpleasant accident if it is in an unexpected place.

It is most important to measure accurately as you do not wish to make more holes than necessary. The rule here is to measure twice, and drill once! Mark the spots you intend to drill with colored crayon.

Then, holding the drill at right angles to the wall, maintain a light pressure when drilling. Drill in approximately 1½ inches. (You can mark this measurement on your drill bit with tape, or move the bit into the drill to the correct length.) Then insert the wall anchor and, holding the bracket in position, put in the screw. Do not tighten until both screws are in position.

When attaching to a wooden house, post or fence, carry out the same procedure but without wall anchors.

How to Put Up a Window Box

Many window boxes will sit securely on deep sills, but as they are so heavy, it is still important to fasten them to the sill. If the box is wooden, you can use angle brackets at the front or sides, drilling and screwing these to secure the box. Otherwise, a length of decorative cast iron along the front of the sill makes an attractive safety option. Again mark first with a crayon, and drill and screw the cast iron on, using wall anchors if necessary.

Fixing a window box

1 *Hang U-shaped brackets (bought to fit the window box) where there is no sill. Fix securely into the wall, using screws and anchors of sufficient strength. Then screw the front of the window box to the brackets.*

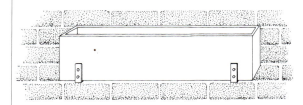

2 *If the box is to sit on a sill, attach L-shaped brackets to the base of the sill with the fronts projecting upward. Sit the box on the brackets, and screw them onto the front of the box.*

Some sills slope, and here you will need to place wedges beneath the box to insure that it is level.

For windows that do not have sills, you can put up window boxes underneath the window, secured by brackets below. Installation is much the same as when putting up shelves.

> ### YOU WILL NEED
> a level · a measuring tape
> a crayon or pencil
> 2 brackets for a box up to
> 3 feet long
> 3 brackets for a box up to
> 5 feet long
> 4 screws and wall anchors per bracket
> window box liner or crockery
> and plastic

Begin by marking in pencil where the box is to be hung. Then, spacing the brackets evenly along the bottom, mark where holes are to be drilled. Draw lines between the marks, and check that they are in a straight line. Adjust where necessary. Drill holes using the correct size of bit for the screws. Place the brackets in position, and insert the screws halfway. When all screws are in, tighten up evenly.

Small plastic window boxes, such as those used for children's boxes, can rest on two screws secured into a fence or wall. Here, you are unlikely to require wall anchors.

Hanging Basket Liners

The first hanging baskets were made of twisted wire lined with sphagnum moss and filled with a peat-based or multi-purpose compost. For a large number of gardeners, this is still the preferred method as such baskets have a natural appearance, although today's wire baskets are usually plastic-coated.

Many gardeners now include a polyethylene liner with slits in it, or a saucer to aid water retention. Various other devices also help to prevent waterlogging or drying out.

Foam, recycled "whalehide" paper, fabric and coconut-fiber liners are available with overlapping flaps, and can be cut to fit any size of basket. These are usually available as overlapping petals, and planting through the slits of these liners enables you to cover the bottom of the basket.

Rigid cardboard liners are made of a compressed paper substance that is biodegradable, but will not last more than one year. They hold water well, but you cannot plant through the sides unless you punch holes in the liner.

Solid-plastic hanging baskets are becoming more popular, particularly those with a false bottom or reservoir for conserving water. This overcomes one of the greatest problems encountered with hanging baskets – infrequent watering. It is not possible to plant through the sides, however, unless there are ready-made holes, so the use of trailing plants to disguise large areas of plastic is important.

Drainage Materials

Some window boxes, such as the more expensive teak varieties, come with plastic liners. It is worth coating all wooden window boxes with a wood preservative before planting. Most window boxes planned for outdoor use, including those made of terracotta, plastic, stone and composites, will not require a liner, but should have drainage

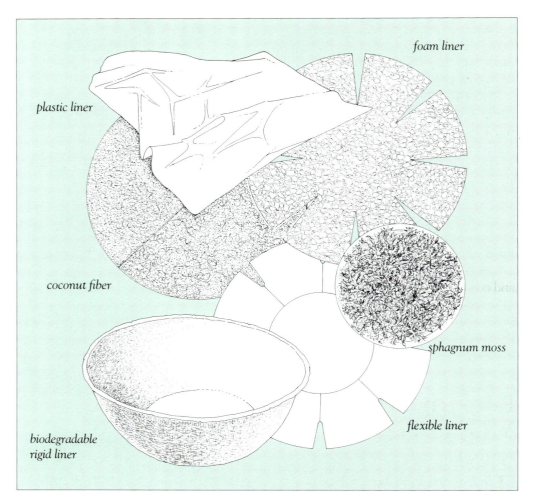

foam liner

plastic liner

coconut fiber

sphagnum moss

flexible liner

biodegradable rigid liner

holes drilled into the bottom if there are none already. These holes should be covered with a layer of crockery.

These broken-up terracotta pots are used to cover the drainage holes in window boxes. This prevents compost from being washed away. Large pebbles can also be used.

Some plants, such as herbs, alpines and bulbs, need a well-drained environment, and will benefit from a layer of horticultural gravel over the crockery. Gravel is also mixed into the compost in the ratio 50:50, and used as a top layer around alpines to prevent them from rotting.

Compost

A peat-based mixture is mainly used for hanging baskets that will be supporting plants for only one season. Peat-based compost is lightweight, contains added nutrients, and is particularly good at retaining water. The nutrients tend to be washed out by frequent watering, but this can be countered by regular feeding.

A multi-purpose potting compost is also suitable, but weighs rather more. A compost designed for hanging baskets is likely to contain water-retaining gel and a slow-release fertilizer.

Peat substitutes, such as coir fiber, are now being introduced as the concern of environmentalists about the depletion of natural peat bogs increases.

A soil-based mixture (multi-purpose compost), containing all necessary nutrients and trace elements, is usually used in window boxes that are intended to last for more than one season, such as those containing small shrubs and alpines.

Ericaceous compost is necessary for lime-hating plants, such as hydrangeas, heathers, conifers and azaleas. Generally, this is best mixed with peat and coarse sand in the proportions 3:2:1.

Some specialty composts will contain small granules of Perlite or vermiculite, or tiny polystyrene balls. These are included to improve drainage, and have no nutritional value.

Looking After Your Flowers

Watering

This is one of the most critical areas with hanging baskets and window boxes as, if the root ball of a plant has dried out, it will prove very difficult to revive.

Watering is best carried out in the cooler part of the day, usually the morning or evening. Generally, the plants need to be in shade when you water, as water magnifies the sun's rays, and can cause scorching of leaves and petals. Try to avoid getting water on leaves or petals.

In damp weather in winter, watering once weekly is all that is required. Never water when the temperature is at freezing or below as the roots will freeze, and be permanently damaged. In spring,

water every few days depending on how warm and dry it is. Check the soil condition by pushing a finger deep into the compost in the box or basket. Do not assume that because the surface is damp, the rest of the compost will be too. In summer you need to water daily, especially on hot days when you may need to water twice or even three times if your basket is in a sunny position.

Use a watering can if you have only one or two baskets. The use of a sprinkling rose on the can will prevent plants from being damaged. Let the basket absorb as much as half the amount of water in the can.
If you can water the baskets on the ground, so much the better. If the water runs straight through, the compost may have dried out around the root balls of the individual plants. If this happens, water again ten minutes later, and again ten minutes after to help the compost become more absorbent again.

If you have a number of containers and baskets, a hose with a wand is the easiest way to water. A wand is a rigid hose extension with an on-off switch, which enables you to reach into high baskets without spraying water everywhere. Many hoses have a twist end which works as an on-off switch too.

To make watering baskets easier, you can buy a pulley attachment to bring the basket down for watering. These are sold in garden centers.

Another product now widely available is water-retaining gel which is available in granule form. This is mixed with water, and added to the compost when planting.

Should you discover that a basket has dried out, soak the whole basket in a

deep bucket of water, holding it under until air bubbles stop rising. Do not feed the basket until the soil has been moist for a few days.

A hand-held sprayer will give plants a quick pick-me-up, but is no substitute for watering with a watering can or hose.

Alpines should be watered carefully in between the plants as the crowns of these plants do not like to be wet. You must use a watering can without a rose.

Herbs need less water than many other plants – not surprising when one considers their Mediterranean origins. Twice weekly should be adequate unless the weather is especially hot.

Feeding

There are two basic methods of feeding. You can use a slow-release fertilizer which is mixed in with the compost when planting, or a liquid or powder feed which is mixed in when watering.

If you choose to add feed when watering, you know exactly when the fertilizer is being applied. If you normally water by hose, you may wish to buy a special hose feed attachment which releases a small amount of fertilizer each time you press a trigger. Alternatively, you could revert to using a watering can for occasional feeding when watering.

Most nurseries and garden centers now include slow-release fertilizer granules when planting baskets. Hanging basket compost often comes with fertilizer already mixed in, so you will not need to fertilize again for a few weeks after planting.

If you choose to feed your baskets or boxes when watering, this should generally be done once a week. If you decide on a certain day of the week, you will be able to remember whether it has been done or not. Too much feed can damage plants, but most manufacturers are aware of this, and are fairly conservative about the amounts they recommend.

Pests and Problems

One of the nice things about hanging baskets and window boxes is that, because they are off the ground, they don't tend to suffer so much from the common problem of slugs and snails, which can inflict a great deal of damage. However, there are still insects and fungi which can cause problems, and, should your plants look unhealthy, one of the first things to establish is what is wrong. The guide to symptoms given here should help.

Careful watering is particularly crucial on hot summer days as, if the roots are totally dry, they will not revive – you can only remove the plant, and start again.

This is sometimes the easiest solution with diseased plants. The speedy removal of one plant can prevent the further spread of an infection, although sprays are often quickly effective. There is now a move toward the use of organic or rather simple soap sprays which do not involve using unnecessarily strong chemicals, although you may occasionally need to use a particular insecticide as specified.

Speedy treatment

Most of us are reluctant to spray, but there are times when a serious disease or pest attack threatens. Aphids and caterpillars can cause severe damage. If this happens, select the right product – ask for advice at your garden center, and read the instructions carefully. Do not make the solution stronger than recommended, and never use a spray can which has previously contained weedkiller. Choose a time when the weather is calm and cloudy, preferably the evening. Use a fine spray, and spray until it is dripping from the leaves. Wash out the equipment, and also wash your hands and face after spraying. Store the package in a safe place, well-labeled, and out of the reach of children and pets.

Plants that have been sprayed will benefit from a foliar feed, i.e., a liquid feed solution that is sprayed onto the leaves rather than put in the compost. This is one way to speed their recovery, and promote healthy growth.

◄ Rust: *raised red, orange or brown spots. Commonly seen on geraniums, snapdragons, sweet williams and chrysanthemums. Treatment: remove affected leaves. Spray with suitable fungicide.*

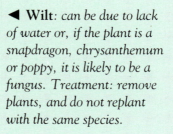

◄ Wilt: *can be due to lack of water or, if the plant is a snapdragon, chrysanthemum or poppy, it is likely to be a fungus. Treatment: remove plants, and do not replant with the same species.*

▼ Leaf miner: *white winding tunnels on marigold and chrysanthemum leaves which eventually turn brown. Treatment: destroy affected leaves. Spray the plant with fungicide.*

► Cold damage: *frosts will cause leaves to curl and wilt – when they open the leaf will be yellow or even white. Treatment: remove affected leaves. Cover plants with protective fleece during cold nights.*

► Powdery mildew: *white surface to leaves caused by overcrowding and insufficient water. A disease seen on verbena, nigella and chrysanthemums. Treatment: spray with fungicide weekly.*

Pests: Symptoms and Cures

SIGNS TO LOOK FOR	PROBLEM	SOLUTION
Yellowing leaves	Overwatering	Water only once a week in winter, adjust according to shade in summer
Browning leaves	Underwatering	Water up to 3 times a day in hot spots and dry spells
Brown areas between leaf veins	Eelworm on phlox, asters, larkspur, calceolaria, chrysanthemum, zinnia and begonia	Pick off affected leaves
Wilt	If soil is moist, could be a soil fungus on antirrhinum, aster, sweet pea or poppy	Remove plant; change compost
Gray mold (*Botrytis*) spots first, rotting occurs later	Humid weather	Pick off moldy flowers and leaves. Spray with fungicide
Ragged petals	Whitefly or aphids on petunia, clarkia, zinnia; earwigs	Shake blooms; spray and place an inverted flowerpot nearby
Distorted buds	Greenfly, blackfly (aphids); warm, dry weather	Use one of the many available sprays early on (organic or chemical)
Large holes in leaves	Caterpillars, woodlice, slugs and snails	Use a long-lasting insecticide; slug pellets
White tracks on the leaves (leaf miner)	Moth and fly larvae on columbines and chrysanthemums	Treat with a chemical spray
Powdery mildew	Fungi growing on begonias, chrysanthemums	Spray from early spring
Rust spots	Fungus on snapdragons, sweet williams, geraniums	Spray plants from early spring or destroy

Plant Lists

This listing gives details of the most commonly grown plants used for hanging baskets and window boxes.

Alyssum, sweet (*Alyssum*)
- clumps of tiny flowers in white, pink, red and purple
- flowers late spring and summer
- well-drained potting compost
- full sun
- deadhead regularly
- very easy to grow

Artemisia absinthium
- attractive silver-gray foliage
- tiny yellow flowers spring to late summer
- leaves look best during summer months
- moist, well-drained potting compost
- full sun for foliage color

Aster (*Aster*)
- daisy-like hardy perennials, mainly purples and pinks
- daisy-like fall flowers
- rich well-drained potting mixture
- sun or semi-shade
- choose low-growing varieties

Begonia (*Begonia semperflorens*)
- vibrant flowers in pink, red, yellow or white
- summer-flowering with attractive green or brown leaves
- humus-rich (acid) potting mixture

- partial shade or shady site
- keep well watered, avoid splashing leaves
- can be kept over winter away from frosts
- feed weekly

Bergenia (elephant's ears) (*Bergenia*)
- large, shiny leathery leaves; tiny pink flower clusters
- hardy evergreen perennial with late summer, fall and winter flowers
- poor, well-drained potting mixture
- sun or shade

Bidens aurea
- yellow, daisy-like flowers on wiry stems
- bushy trailing habit particularly suits hanging baskets
- plant in spring, flowers all summer
- well-drained potting compost
- prefers full sun but do not let dry out
- increasingly popular

Brachycome (*Brachycome*)
- small, daisy-like purple flowers
- summer-flowering
- good for hanging baskets
- well-drained potting compost
- prefers sunny site

Bugle (*Ajuga reptans*)
- attractive foliage plant; dark green/purple leaves
- tiny blue flowers on 8-inch spikes from mid-spring to early summer
- rich, moist potting compost
- full sun to light shade
- hardy

Box (*Buxus sempervirens*)
- hardy evergreen shrub
- tiny leaves, compact growth
- well-drained soil
- sun or shade
- can be clipped into shapes

Cabbage, ornamental (*Brassica*)
- attractive fall/winter foliage; pink, white and dark red varieties
- plant in the fall to last until spring
- prefers acidic potting mixture
- sunny site

Cacti (*Cacti*)
- succulent foliage plant, often with spikes or hairs
- flowers in summer, in winter also indoors
- free-draining compost
- sunny spot preferable
- hardy, can withstand drying out

Calceolaria (*Calceolaria*)
- bold flowers in purple, pink and white
- flowers all summer long
- moist but well-drained compost
- sun or shade
- keep well watered

Campanula (bellflower, Canterbury bell) (*Campanula*)
- delicate, blue, bell-shaped flowers
- flowers early to late summer
- moist but well-drained soil
- sun or shade
- trailing varieties have a long flowering period

Celosia (*Celosia*)
- brightly colored "feather duster" plumes

- summer-flowering
- well-drained compost
- sunny spot away from wind
- flowers are red, orange, yellow and pink

Chives (*Allium schoenoprasum*)
- herb with green fronds and pink flowers
- plant in spring for summer growth
- multi-purpose potting mixture
- full sun
- remove flowers to encourage foliage

Chrysanthemum (*Chrysanthemum*)
- large, daisy-like flowerheads, mainly orange, yellow and white
- late-summer- and fall-flowering
- lightly limed soil is best
- sunny spot
- deadhead regularly
- spray against greenfly

Cineraria (senecio or dusty miller) (*Senecio*)
- large, silver-gray, intricate leaf
- plant in spring for a long summer show
- any well-drained compost
- needs full sun for silvery leaves
- survives most mild winters
- remove small yellow flowers

Clary Sage (*Salvia*)
- purple, pink and lilac spires of flowers
- summer-flowering
- chalky (alkaline) compost
- sunny site
- do not let dry out

Coleus (*Coleus blumei*)
- large, colorful leaves in

- hardy evergreen; red berries in winter
- well-drained potting mixture
- sun or shade
- trailing and climbing varieties available

Hosta (*Hosta*)
- large attractive leaves, some variegated
- one or two tall flower spires in summer
- moist, well-drained soil
- sun or shade
- some varieties are scented

Houseleek (*Sempervivum*)
- rosette of succulent pointed leaves
- summer flowers; use in alpine box
- shallow, well-drained potting compost containing gravel
- sunny position

Hyacinth (*Hyacinthus*)
- thick spikes of scented flowers; pink, blue and white most popular
- spring-flowering bulbs
- well-drained potting compost
- sunny or semi-shady site
- dwarf varieties available

Hydrangea (*Hydrangea*)
- a hardy shrub with full flowerheads
- large summer flowerheads dry well
- prefers rich, moist, but well-drained, potting compost
- sun or semi-shade
- prefers ericaceous soil

Impatiens (*Impatiens*)
- prolific flowers in white, pink, red, lilac, orange
- flowers all summer long

- moist, well-drained potting mixture
- sun or shade
- keep watered in dry spells

Iris, dwarf (*Iris reticulata*)
- striking blue flower on strong stem
- plant bulbs in the fall for late-winter, early-spring flowers
- keep compost moist through winter
- sunny situation, can withstand cold
- dwarf varieties suit window boxes

Ivy (*Hedera helix*)
- useful foliage plant with attractive leaf shape, some variegated
- hardy evergreen, can be used year round
- moist soil conditions
- shade-loving
- trailing varieties can be used to cover basket chains and handles

Juniper (spreading fir) (*Juniperus*)
- needle-like foliage, low-growing
- evergreen; bright berries midwinter
- prefers acid soil
- sunny site if possible

Lady's mantle (*Alchemilla mollis*)
- tiny powdery-yellow flowers; attractive yellow green foliage
- flowers all summer
- well-drained compost
- sunny situation
- particularly suits window boxes and baskets

Laurel, spotted (*Aucuba japonica*)
- attractive, large, spotted, mid-green leaves
- evergreen
- standard potting compost
- sun or shade
- easy to grow

Lavender (*Lavandula*)
- scented gray green leaves; some varieties silvery
- purple flowers in summer
- rich, well-drained compost
- prefers a sunny site

Lemon balm (*Melissa officinalis*)
- attractive, scented foliage
- white flowers mid-summer
- light, well-drained compost
- full sun
- remove flowers for increased foliage

Leucothoe (*Leucothoe*)
- attractive foliage plant; leaves turn red in fall
- evergreen shrub, good for fall/winter color; white flowers in spring and early summer
- moist, acidic (ericaceous) potting mixture
- shade or semi-shade

Lily, African (*Agapanthus*)
- blue or white, delicate, bell-shaped flowers
- summer-flowering
- moist potting mixture, well drained
- sunny situation
- deadhead regularly

Lily of the valley (*Convallaria*)
- delicate white, winter blooms
- fragrant, early-spring flowers

- moist potting mixture
- sun or semi-shade
- grow from rhizomes

Lobelia (*Lobelia*)
- popular, bushy, trailing plant in blues, purple and, recently, dark red varieties
- flowers for one season only, from early to late summer
- moist, well-drained mixture
- sun or semi-shade
- do not let dry out

Maidenhair fern (*Adiantum*)
- fern with delicate, attractive foliage
- year-round foliage in moist conditions
- damp, neutral to acid potting mixture
- shady or semi-shady site
- do not let dry out

Maple, Japanese (*Acer palmatum*)
- hardy shrub with unusual dark leaves
- deciduous
- rich, well-drained potting compost
- sun or semi-shade
- container restricts growth, so it is suitable for boxes

Marguerite, golden (chamomile) (*Anthemis*)
- daisy-like flowers in white and yellow
- summer-flowering
- parsley-like foliage
- well-drained potting compost
- sunny position
- deadhead regularly

Marigold pot; French (*Calendula; Tagetes*)
- orange, cream and yellow flowers in various sizes
- spring, summer and fall flowers

107

- any well-drained potting compost
- sunny situation preferred
- deadhead regularly

Mint (*Mentha*)
- strong-smelling herb; leaves used for mint sauce
- best from late spring to late summer
- any potting compost but not too dry
- full sun to very light shade
- can be invasive, keep in pot

Monkey flower (*Mimulus*)
- pretty, bell-like flowers with spotted "monkey" face in yellow, orange and red
- summer-flowering
- moist compost
- prefers sunny situation
- deadhead regularly

Nasturtiums (*Tropaeolum*)
- orange, red and yellow annuals and perennials
- edible flowers in late summer
- well-drained potting compost
- sunny site

Nemesia (*Nemesia*)
- prolific small flowers in a wide variety of colors
- summer-flowering, short-lived if dry
- lime-free potting compost
- sun or light shade
- keep well watered
- easy to grow from seed

Nephrolepis fern (*Nephrolepis*)
- attractive, arching fronds of foliage
- year-round leaf interest
- rich, moist potting mixture
- light sun to deep shade

Nicotiana, see tobacco plant

Oxalis (*Oxalis adenophylla*)
- cloverlike leaf; small yellow flowers in clusters
- flowers late spring to early fall
- full sun to light shade
- light, open, sandy soil
- water and feed frequently

Palm, see cordyline

Pansy (*Viola*)
- prolific easy-to-grow flowers in many shades
- summer- and winter-flowering varieties
- well-drained, moist compost
- any situation, sun or shade
- deadhead regularly

Parsley (*Petroselinum*)
- herb with attractive, fine foliage, used for cooking and decoration
- plant late spring for summer growth; dies with frost
- moist, well-drained soil
- sunny site
- trim regularly to encourage growth

Pelargonium (*Pelargonium*)
See also Geranium
- easy-to-grow bold flowers, some with scented leaves, many varieties available
- plant after frosts for summer-flowering; can be year-round if kept in a warm and sunny spot in winter, i.e., greenhouse or windowsill inside
- dryish, well-drained potting mixture
- more flowers in a sunny site
- take cuttings in late summer for propagation

Penstemon, beard tongue (*Penstemon*)
- delicate, foxglove-like blooms in pinks, reds and purples
- early- to late-summer-flowering
- rich, well-drained potting compost
- prefers light shade; tolerates full sun

Periwinkle (*Vinca*)
- evergreen shrub with glossy leaves
- purple flowers in spring
- well-drained potting mixture
- sun or shade
- attractive trailing foliage

Petunias, multiflora, floribunda, grandiflora (*Petunia*)
- prolific flower trumpets in striking red, purple, pink and white with striped and starred hybrids
- non-stop summer to fall flowers
- well-drained potting mixture
- sun or semi-shade
- watch for new trailing hybrid – "Surfinia"
- some lightly scented

Phlox (*Phlox*)
- tightly massed flowerheads in white, yellow, pink and purple
- flowers late spring to late summer
- any well-drained potting compost
- sunny site
- choose dwarf varieties

Pick-a-back plant (*Tolmiea*)
- attractive, pale green foliage, with small leaves growing just above larger ones

- can survive year round if climate is not severe
- well-drained, slightly acid potting compost
- shade or semi-shade
- plantlets can be propagated

Pinks (*Dianthus*)
- tufted flowers in pink and white; scented and variegated varieties available
- hardy evergreen foliage; summer flowers
- well-drained potting compost
- sunny site
- deadhead regularly

Plectranthus (*Plectranthus*)
- attractive trailing foliage
- tender perennials, some evergreen
- moist potting compost
- sun or semi-shade
- cut back straggly growth

Polyanthus (*Primula*)
- cross between cowslip and primrose with masses of bright blooms in clusters on stalks; many shades available
- early-spring-flowering
- any moist potting compost
- semi-shade preferable

Poppy (*Papaver*)
- delicate blooms on fine stems; yellows, reds and pinks
- colorful summer flowers
- light, well-drained soil
- sun or semi-shade
- alpine varieties do well

Portulaca (sun plant) (*Portulaca*)
- succulent, fleshy-leaved plants with brightly colored flowers
- summer-flowering
- well-drained sandy soil
- needs full sun

Primrose (*Primula*)
● popular spring plant with long, wide leaves and bright, rewarding flowers
● plant in late winter/early spring for flowers early to mid-spring
● moist, rich potting compost
● light to medium shade
● yellow varieties are scented

Ranunculus (Persian buttercup) (*Ranunculus asiaticus*)
● brightly colored peony-like flower with masses of petals in yellow, deep and pale pink, white with pink edging
● late-spring flowers
● moist, but well-drained, potting mixture
● full sun to semi-shade
● grown from tubers

Rock rose, see helianthemum

Rosa (*Rosa*)
● attractive clusters of flower petals, thorny stems; some fragrant
● flowers spring and summer
● moist, well-drained compost
● sunny site
● choose miniature varieties for containers

Rudbeckia (*Rudbeckia*)
● large, daisy-like flowers in red, orange and yellow
● late-summer-, early-fall-flowering
● well-drained potting compost
● sun or light shade
● choose dwarf varieties

Sage (*Salvia*)
● hardy evergreen herb with soft gray green foliage

● summer and fall flowers
● well-drained potting mixture
● sunny site
● some have aromatic or variegated foliage

Santolina (*Santolina*)
● hardy evergreen shrub with scented silver foliage
● yellow summer flowers
● well-drained potting mixture
● sunny site
● good for year-round interest

Saponaria, see tumbling ted

Scabious (*Scabiosa*)
● hardy plant with pincushion-like, pale, cornflower-blue flowers
● late-summer-flowering
● rich, well-drained potting mixture (not acidic)
● sunny site
● some scented varieties

Scilla (*Scilla*)
● spikes of small blue flowers
● spring-flowering bulbs
● well-drained potting compost
● sun or semi-shade

Sedum (*Sedum*)
● attractive, fleshy or succulent foliage
● summer to fall flowers
● well-drained potting mixture
● sunny site
● do not overwater

Senecio (*Senecio*)
● attractive silver leaves
● daisy-like flowers in spring, summer and fall
● well-drained potting mixture
● sun or semi-shade

Silene (*Silene*)
● annuals and perennials
● flowers in late spring to the end of summer
● well-drained, gravelly compost
● sun or semi-shade
● do not let become waterlogged

Sisyrinchium (*Sisyrinchium*)
● yellow flowers on upright spikes
● flowers mid- to late summer
● light, well-drained, humus-rich compost
● full sun
● grows to 2 feet tall

Skimmia (*Skimmia*)
● evergreen shrub; red berries in the fall
● sweet-scented white/pink flowers in spring
● moisture-retaining potting compost
● sun or shade

Snapdragon (*Antirrhinum*)
● flower trumpets in red, yellow, orange and brown
● spring to fall flowers
● rich, well-drained potting compost
● flowers open in sun
● deadhead regularly
● choose dwarf varieties where possible

Snowberries (*Symphoricarpos*)
● white, globular fruit; evergreen foliage
● spring flowers; winter fruit
● moist potting compost
● semi-shade
● fruits are poisonous

Snow-in-summer (*Cerastium tomentosum*)
● hardy, flowering plant with pretty silver foliage

● prolific white flowers late spring to early summer
● any potting compost
● full sun
● trim regularly

Sorrel (*Rumex*)
● red-green herb with upright, feathery foliage
● plant in spring for summer use
● well-drained potting compost
● full sun

Spurge (*Euphorbia*)
● foliage plants with attractive fleshy leaves
● spring flowers
● moist, but well-drained, compost
● sun or semi-shade
● can irritate skin

Stocks (*Matthiola*)
● multiple, scented blooms on spires; many shades available
● flowering mid-spring and mid-summer
● well-drained potting compost, not acidic
● sun or light shade
● lingering fragrance

Strawberry, wild (*Fragaria*)
● hardy plant with attractive trailing foliage, white or pink flowers and edible summer fruit
● plant mid-fall to mid-spring for flowers in late spring and fruit throughout summer months
● well-drained potting compost
● sunny site
● cut away unwanted runners

Sunflower (*Helianthus*)
● bright, giant, daisy-like flowers in yellow, red and orange, with brown centers

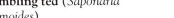

- mid-summer-flowering
- any potting compost
- full sun
- compact varieties available

Surfinia, see petunia

Swedish ivy
- attractive green and white trailing foliage
- perennial
- well-drained potting compost
- full sun or light shade

Sweet william (*Dianthus barbatus*)
- flattened heads of sweet-smelling pink flowers
- flowers in late spring and summer
- well-drained potting compost, not acidic
- sunny situation
- dwarf varieties available

Tarragon, French (*Artemisia dranunculus*)
- spiky upright herb; aromatic gray green foliage
- plant in spring for summer-long use
- well-drained potting compost
- sunny situation
- trim to promote growth

Thrift (*Armeria maritima*)
- evergreen alpine
- deep pink flowers in early to late summer
- well-drained potting compost
- full sun
- does not like wet winters

Thuja (*Thuja*)
- conifer with needle-like foliage in shades of green, gray and yellow
- acidic soil
- any situation
- do not let dry out

Thyme (*Thymus*)
- hardy evergreen herb with attractive, scented leaves
- white flowers in summer
- moist, well-drained potting mixture
- sunny site
- remove flowers for foliage growth

Tobacco plant (*Nicotiana*)
- fairly hardy, tall foliage with prolific flowers
- long-lasting summer flowers
- rich, well-drained potting compost
- likes semi-shade or shade
- some varieties scented
- can grow to 2 feet

Tomato, tumbler
- trailing plants with cherry-size tomatoes
- shoots do not need pinching out
- small yellow flowers in early summer, fruits mid- to late summer
- rich, moist compost
- sunny site
- keep well fed and watered

Tradescantia (*Tradescantia*)
- very hardy, trailing foliage, some pink-edged
- houseplants that do well outside in summer
- well-drained potting mixture – not fussy
- sun or semi-shade
- bring in before first frosts

Tulip (*Tulipa*)
- hardy perennial grown from bulb
- colorful spring flowers
- well-drained alkaline potting mixture
- sun or semi-shade
- choose dwarf varieties

Tumbling ted (*Saponaria ocymoides*)
- profuse, rose-pink flowers
- flowers in mid-summer to early fall
- thrives on well-drained compost
- sunny site
- compact, prostrate, tumbling growth

Verbena (*Verbena*)
- colorful trailing clusters of summer flowers, mostly pinks and purples, good for hanging baskets
- summer-flowering
- well-drained potting mixture
- sun or semi-shade
- some scented varieties

Veronica (*Veronica*)
- attractive spires of blue or pink flowers
- mid- to late-summer-flowering
- any potting compost
- full sun to light shade
- miniature and alpine varieties available

Violet, sweet (*Viola odorata*)
- small-headed, fragrant pansy
- different varieties flower all year round
- well-drained potting mixture
- any site, sun or shade
- *V. labradorica* is particularly suitable for containers
- deadhead regularly

Wallflower (*Cheiranthus cheiri*)
- colorful massed petals on upright stems; many shades available, red and yellow most commonly seen

- spring-flowering
- well-drained alkaline potting compost – adding garden lime (chalk) will help
- sunny spot
- choose shorter varieties

INDEX

ACKNOWLEDGMENTS

The author would like to thank the following people for their help on *Window Boxes and Hanging Baskets*:

Frankie Annis, Graham Wallis, Mr J. Wilson and Mr S. Curtis for horticultural help and advice. Also Mr and Mrs M. Fordham, Mr and Mrs J. Mustoe, Miss R. Amy, Mr and Mrs B. Barham, Mrs L. Allen and Mr P. Hiscocks, Mr and Mrs R. McLellan, Mr and Mrs R. Osborn, Mr and Mrs I. Fletcher, Mr and Mrs A. Knight, Mr and Mrs A. Tilbury, Mr and Mrs J. Wilson, Mr and Mrs Woore, Mrs J. Harper, Mr and Mrs Melville, Mr and Mrs C. Arnold, Mr P. Garnier, Mr and Mrs Huxley, Mrs H. Yeomans, Mrs J. Lewis, Mrs L. Fairholm, Mrs S. Ravenhill, Mrs W. Ellard, Dr E. Biggs, Mr and Mrs Mendelsohn, Saffron Walden nursery school and all the residents of Hampton, Middlesex for kindly allowing us to photograph in their gardens.

Project editor Gill MacLennan for all her assistance with planting and photography, gardening editor Lesley Young and Maggie Aldred who art directed with care and precision. Also John Clarke at Garson Farm Garden Centre in Esher and Liz Gage, Caroline Owen, Sally Spicer and Dot and Caroline of Scotsdale Garden Centre, Great Shelford, Cambridge, for the supply of plants, containers and advice.

Special thanks to photographers Spike Powell and Glyn Barney for their enthusiasm and commitment.

Chelsea Flower Show Exhibitors: Hermitage Horticultural Society, The Allotment Holders Association, The Harrow Show, Shipdham Horticultural Society, The Royal Hospital, Berkshire College of Agriculture, Brightling Flower Show Society, Horton Cum Studley Horticultural Society, Kingston Horticultural Society.

Specialist Suppliers
Containers
Webbs, Unit 2, 15 Station Road, Knebworth, Stevenage, Herts SG3 6AP
Scotsdale Garden Centre, Cambridge Road, Great Shelford, Cambridge CB2 5JT
The Terracotta Shop, 8 Moorfield Road, Duxford, Cambridgeshire

Plants
F. Annis, 51 North Road, Abington, Cambridgeshire
Grace's Farm Shop, nr Thaxted, Essex
Ickleton Trout Farm & Nursery, Frogge Street, Ickleton, Cambridgeshire
Springwell Nurseries, Josephs Farm, Springwell, Little Chesterford, Essex
Siskin Plants (alpines) Woodbridge, Suffolk
Squires Garden Centre, Sixth Cross Road, Twickenham, Middlesex
Putney Garden Centre, Upper Richmond Road, Putney SW15
Garson Farm Garden Centre, Winterdown Road, West End, Esher, Surrey

Also for loan of faux lead window box
Capital Garden Products, Gibbs Reed Barn, Pashley Road, Ticehurst, East Sussex TN5 7HE